FIRST EDITION

*To my father, who always
wanted me to write a book,*

*My mother, who always
made me feel like I could,*

*Melanie, who married me—the
greatest stroke of good fortune of my life,*

*and my son Harry, who will surely
write books much better than this one
whenever he wants to.*

SECOND EDITION

*To my big brother, Phil,
who was a mensch his whole life.*

CONTENTS

About the Second Edition

Since *Don't Make Me Think* was first published nearly five years ago, people have been wonderful about the book.

I get lots of lovely email. You can't imagine how nice it is to start your morning with someone you've never met telling you that they enjoyed something that you did. (I recommend it highly.)

Even nicer is the fact that people seem to like the book for the same reasons I do. For instance:

> Many people appreciate the fact that it's short. (Some have told me that they actually read it on a plane ride, which was one of my stated objectives for the first edition; the record for "fastest read" seems to be about two hours.)

> A gratifying number of people have said that they liked the book because it practices what it preaches, in the writing and the design.

> Some people said it made them laugh out loud, which I really appreciated. (One reader said that I made her laugh so hard that milk came out of her nose. How can something like that help but make you feel that your time has been well spent?)

But the most satisfying thing has been people saying that it helped them get their job done better.

But what have you done for us lately?

It only took about a year after the book appeared for people to start asking me when I was going to do a second edition.

For a long time, I really resisted the idea. I liked the book the way it was and thought it worked well, and since it was about design principles and not technology, I didn't think it was likely to be out of date anytime soon.

Usually I'd pull the consultant/therapist trick of asking them what *they* would change, and the answer was almost always, "Well, I guess you could update the examples." Some people would point out that some of the sites in the examples didn't even exist anymore.

But the fact is, many of the sites in the book were already gone by the time it hit the bookstores. (Remember, it came out right before the Internet bubble burst.) The fact that the sites weren't around didn't make the examples any less clear.

Other people would say, "Well, you could talk about the things about the Web that have changed." It's true; some things about the Web *have* changed in the last few years. Some of the changes were good:

> More good sites to copy from

> Cascading Style Sheets (CSS) that actually work

> Useful conventions like printer-friendly pages and Amazon.com's What's this?

> Google as the starting point for all actions

> The swing in business models from banner ads (for things I don't want) to Google ads (for things I actually might want)

> Hardly anyone uses frames anymore

...and some not so good:

> Pop-ups

> Phishing

But these changes didn't make me feel a need to update the book, which is about design principles, not specifics of technology or implementation.

And there was one other problem: I was very proud of how short the book was. It took a lot of work, but it was an important part of the "practices what it preaches" business. If I was going to add any new material, I'd have to throw some of the existing stuff overboard, and I thought it all worked pretty well.

So, what are we doing here?

One of the nicest fringe benefits of the book for me is that I've been able to spend time teaching workshops.

In the workshops, I try to do the same thing I did in the book: show people what I think about when I do a usability review of a Web site.

And since everyone who comes to the workshops has already read the book, naturally I had to come up with different examples to make the same points, and different ways of explaining the same things. I also get to do a lot of reviews of different kinds of sites, because everyone who comes to the workshop can submit a URL, and during the day I do 12-minute "expert mini-reviews" of some of them, and a live user test of one or two others.

And as anyone who's ever taught anything knows, teaching something is the best way to learn more about it.

So when my publisher started asking about a second edition again last year, I actually thought about what a second edition might be like. And while I still felt there wasn't much I'd change or delete from the first edition, I realized I did have some other things I could write about that might be helpful.

Like what?

The new material mostly falls into three categories:

> **Oh, *now* I get it.** Teaching the workshops has given me many chances to think through what's in the book. There are a few things that I've rewritten slightly because I think I understand them a little better now, or I have a better way to explain them.

> **Help! My boss wants me to _____.** A lot of the questions people ask in my workshops amount to "I know the right thing to do in this case, but my boss/client/stakeholders insist that I do the wrong thing. How can I convince them otherwise?"

Since many people seem to spend a lot of time trying to fight the same design issues, I thought it might be good to give them some ammunition. So I added Chapter 12, which covers problems like

> My marketing manager insists that we make people provide a lot of unnecessary personal information before they can subscribe to our newsletter, and it doesn't seem to matter to him that 10% of our subscribers now happen to be named "Barney Rubble."

> **The "lost" chapters.** There were two chapters I wanted to include in the first book, but didn't, mostly in the interest of keeping it short. One, Chapter 10, is about the importance of treating users well, and the other, Chapter 11, is about Web accessibility.

I also wanted to update and expand my recommended reading list, since some great books have come out in the past five years.

Five pounds of crackers in a four-pound box

Even though I'd gone from thinking the book was fine just the way it was, thank you, to feeling like I had a lot I wanted to add, I still had one major dilemma: If there wasn't anything I wanted to throw overboard, how could I add new material and still keep the book short enough for an airplane ride read?

Fortunately, at this point, I took my own advice and did a form of user testing: I set up a discussion board and asked readers of the first edition to tell me what I could leave out. And fortunately, the testing did what user testing always does:

> Confirmed some things I already knew

> Taught me some things I didn't know about how people were using the book, and what they valued about it

> Whacked me over the head with a big surprise that let me improve it significantly

The big surprise was the large number of people who suggested moving the chapters on user testing to another book. (Some of them had heard that I was planning to do another book that would cover low-cost/no-cost do-it-yourself user testing in detail, and some said they wouldn't miss the chapters because they didn't plan on doing any testing themselves.)

I'd thought of doing this, but I didn't want to because (a) I thought people would miss them, and (b) I thought it would feel like I was trying to force people to buy the second book. But as soon as I started reading what the users had to say, the solution became obvious: By compressing the three user testing chapters into one slightly shorter one that covers the important points everyone should know about, I could gain twenty more pages to use for new material. And for anyone who wanted the older, longer version, I could make the original chapters available for free on my Web site.[1] Problem solved.

Finally, a few housekeeping notes:

> **The links.** If you want to visit any of the URLs mentioned in the book, you'll find up-to-date links on my site, too. (Just in case any of the sites, well, you know...disappear.)

> **Still not present at time of photo.** The one thing people have asked me about that you still won't find in here is any discussion of Web applications. While a lot of the principles are the same as for Web sites, it's really a topic for a whole other book, and I'm not the person to write it.[2]

Anyway, thanks for all the fish. I hope you find the new bits useful.

See you in five years.

STEVE KRUG
JULY 2005

---

[1] http://www.sensible.com/secondedition

[2] *If that's your area, you might want to take a look at* Web Application Design Handbook: Best Practices for Web-Based Software *by Susan Fowler and Victor Stanwick.*

Foreword >

DON'T MAKE ME THINK AGAIN

ONSIDERING HOW MUCH HAS CHANGED SINCE 2000, WHEN THE first edition of this book was printed, it's amazing that the basic design of the Web has stayed so much the same.

In the early years the platform was volatile. It seemed like features changed every week. We had the browser wars, with Netscape squaring off against all comers and the WC3 bringing out new HTML standards every six months. But then, with the predictable victory of the Redmond *wehrmacht*, everything settled down.

This was a relief for Web designers, who were nearly driven out of their minds by the constant changes in code—and by the fact that we were making it up as we went along.

But relief slowly faded into frustration.

The inflexibility of HTML, the lack of fonts, the adjustability of Web pages that makes design so imprecise, the confusing array of screen resolutions and target browsers (even if they're mostly Explorer)—these factors are all annoying.

Designers' aggravation is compounded by the slow coagulation of a number of restrictive conventions, like the use of banner ads. Not all conventions are bad of course. In fact, users *like* conventions—even if designers find them constraining. For most people, it's hard enough just to get the computer to work.

And while these conventions may change, there is one constant that never changes: human nature. As radical and disruptive a social and commercial force as the Internet has been, it has not yet caused a noticeable mutation in the species.

And since we designers do not, as a rule, come into contact with actual human beings, it is very helpful to know Steve Krug—or at least to have this book—because Steve *does* know users. After more than a decade of this work he continues to look at each Web site like it's the first one. You'll find no buzz words here: just common sense and a friendly understanding of the way we see, the way we think, and the way we read.

The principles Steve shares here are going to stay the same, no matter what happens with the Internet—with web conventions, or the operating system, or bandwidth, or computer power. So pull up a chair and relax.

ROGER BLACK
NEW YORK, JULY 2005

Read me first

THROAT CLEARING AND DISCLAIMERS

WHEN I STARTED TELLING PEOPLE THAT I WAS WRITING A book about how to do what I do, they all asked the same thing: "Aren't you afraid of putting yourself out of a job?"

It's true, I have a great job.

> People ("clients") send me proposed page designs for the new Web site they're building or the URL of the existing site that they're redesigning.

New Home page design A

New Home page design B

Existing site

> I look at the designs or use the site and figure out whether they're easy enough to use (an "expert usability review"). Sometimes I pay other people to try to use the site while I watch ("usability testing").[1]

> I write a report describing the problems that I found that are likely to cause users grief ("usability issues") and suggesting possible solutions.[2]

A usability report

---

[1] *...not to be confused with "voyeurism."*

[2] *Actually, this is one thing that has changed since the first edition. See Chapter 9 for the reason why I've pretty much stopped writing what I now refer to as the "big honking report."*

> I work with the client's Web design team to help them figure out how to fix the problems.

Sometimes we work by phone...

...and sometimes in person

> They pay me.

Being a consultant, I get to work on interesting projects with a lot of nice, smart people, and when we're finished, the sites are better than when we started. I get to work at home most of the time and I don't have to sit in mind-numbing meetings every day or deal with office politics. I get to say what I think, and people usually appreciate it. And I get paid well.

Believe me, I would not lightly jeopardize this way of life.[3]

But the reality is there are so many Web sites in need of help—and so few people who do what I do—that barring a total collapse of the Internet boom,[4] there's very little chance of my running out of work for years.

Suddenly a lot of people with little or no previous experience have been made responsible for big-budget projects that may determine the future of their companies, and they're looking for people to tell them that they're doing it right.

---

[3] *I have an even cushier job now. Since the book came out, I spend a lot of my time teaching workshops, where, unlike consulting, there's no opportuntiy to procrastinate and no homework. At the end of the day, you're done.*

[4] *The boom obviously turned to bust not long after I wrote this (late in 2000). Even so, there are probably more people working on usability now than there were then.*

Graphic designers and developers find themselves responsible for designing interfaces—things like interaction design (what happens next when the user clicks) and information architecture (how everything is organized).

And most people don't have the budget to hire a usability consultant to review their work—let alone have one around all the time.

I'm writing this book for people who can't afford to hire (or rent) someone like me. I would hope that it's also of value to people who work with a usability professional.

At the very least, I hope it can help you avoid some of the endless, circular religious Web design debates that seem to eat up so much time.

It's not rocket surgery™

The good news is that much of what I do is just common sense, and anyone with some interest can learn to do it.

After all, usability really just means making sure that something works well: that a person of average (or even below average) ability and experience can use the thing—whether it's a Web site, a fighter jet, or a revolving door—for its intended purpose without getting hopelessly frustrated.

Like a lot of common sense, though, it's not necessarily obvious until *after* someone's pointed it out to you.[5]

No question: if you can afford to, hire someone like me. But if you can't, I hope this book will enable you to do it yourself (in your copious spare time).

---

[5] *...which is one reason why my consulting business (actually just me and a few well-placed mirrors) is called Advanced Common Sense. "It's not rocket surgery" is my corporate motto.*

Yes, it's a thin book

I've worked hard to keep this book short—hopefully short enough you can read it on a long plane ride. I did this for two reasons:

> **If it's short, it's more likely to actually be used.**[6] I'm writing for the people who are in the trenches—the designers, the developers, the site producers, the project managers, the marketing people, and the people who sign the checks, and for the one-man-band people who are doing it all themselves. Usability isn't your life's work, and you don't have time for a long book.

> **You don't need to know everything.** As with any field, there's a lot you *could* learn about usability. But unless you're a usability professional, there's a limit to how much is *useful* to learn.[7]

---

[6] *There's a good usability principle right there: if something requires a large investment of time—or looks like it will—it's less likely to be used.*

[7] *I've always liked the passage in* A Study in Scarlet *where Dr. Watson is shocked to learn that Sherlock Holmes doesn't know that the earth travels around the sun. Given the finite capacity of the human brain, Holmes explains, he can't afford to have useless facts elbowing out the useful ones:*

> *"What the deuce is it to me? You say that we go round the sun. If we went round the moon it would not make a pennyworth of difference to me or to my work."*

I find that the most valuable contributions I make to each project always come from keeping just a few key usability principles in mind. I think there's a lot more leverage for most people in understanding these principles than in another laundry list of specific do's and don'ts. I've tried to boil down the few things I think everybody involved in building Web sites should know.

Not present at time of photo

Just so you don't waste your time looking for them, here are a few things you *won't* find in this book:

> **"The truth" about the right way to design Web sites.** I've been at this for a long time, long enough to know that there is no one "right" way to design Web sites. It's a complicated process and the real answer to most of the questions that people ask me is "It depends."[8] But I do think that there are a few useful guiding principles it always helps to have in mind, and those are what I'm trying to convey.

> **Discussion of business models.** If history has taught us anything, it's that Internet business models are like buses: If you miss one, all you have to do is wait a little while and another one will come along. I'm no expert when it comes to making money on the Web, and even if I were, whatever I had to say would probably be passé by the time you read it.

> **Predictions for the future of the Web.** Your guess is as good as mine. The only thing I'm sure of is that (a) most of the predictions I hear are almost certainly wrong, and (b) the things that will turn out to be important will come as a surprise, even though in hindsight they'll seem perfectly obvious.

> **Bad-mouthing of poorly designed sites.** If you enjoy people poking fun at sites with obvious flaws, you're reading the wrong book. Designing, building, and maintaining a great Web site isn't easy. It's like golf: a handful of ways to get the ball in the hole, a million ways not to. Anyone who gets it even half right has my admiration.

---

[8] *Jared Spool and his usability consulting cohorts at User Interface Engineering* (www.uie.com) *even have "It depends" T-shirts.*

As a result, you'll find that the sites I use as examples tend to be excellent sites with minor flaws. I think you can learn more from looking at good sites than bad ones.

> **Examples from all kinds of sites.** Most of the examples in the book are from e-commerce sites, but the principles I'm describing apply just as well to my next-door neighbor's vanity page, your daughter's soccer team's site, or your company's intranet. Including illustrations from all the different genres would have resulted in a much larger—and less useful book.

Who's on first?

Throughout the book, I've tried to avoid constant references to "the user" and "users." This is partly because of the tedium factor, but also to try to get you to think about your own experience as a Web user while you're reading—something most of us tend to forget when we've got our Web design hats on. This has led to the following use of pronouns in this book:

> **"I" is me, the author.** Sometimes it's me the usability professional ("I tell my clients…") and sometimes it's me speaking as a Web user ("If I can't find a Search button…"), but it's always me.

> **"You" is you, the reader**—someone who designs, builds, publishes, or pays the bills for a Web site.

> **"We" ("How we really use the Web") is all Web users**, which includes "you" and "I."

I may sidestep these rules occasionally, but hopefully the context will always make it clear who I'm talking about.

Is this trip really necessary?

I could recite some of the usual awe-inspiring statistics about how many umpteen gazillion dollars will be left on the table this year by sites that don't mind their usability P's and Q's.

But given that you're already holding a book about usability in your hands, you probably don't need me to tell you that usability matters. You know from your own experience as a Web user that paying attention to usability means less frustration and more satisfaction for your visitors, and a better chance that you'll see them again.

I think my wife put her finger on the essence of it better than any statistic I've seen:

I hope this book will help you build a better site and—if you can skip a few design arguments—maybe even get home in time for dinner once in a while.

Don't make me think!

KRUG'S FIRST LAW OF USABILITY

People often ask me:

> "What's the most important thing I should do if I
> want to make sure my Web site is easy to use?"

The answer is simple. It's not "Nothing important should ever be more than two clicks away," or "Speak the user's language," or even "Be consistent."

It's...

"Don't make me think!"

I've been telling people for years that this is my first law of usability. And the more Web pages I look at, the more convinced I become.

It's the overriding principle— the ultimate tie breaker when deciding whether something works or doesn't in a Web design. If you have room in your head for only one usability rule, make this the one.[1]

It means that as far as is humanly possible, when I look at a Web page it should be self-evident. Obvious. Self-explanatory.

I should be able to "get it"—what it is and how to use it—without expending any effort thinking about it.

Just how self-evident are we talking about?

Well, self-evident enough, for instance, that your next door neighbor, who has no interest in the subject of your site and who barely knows how to use the Back button, could look at your site's Home page and say, "Oh, it's a ___." (With any luck, she'll say, "Oh, it's a ___. *Neat.*" But that's another subject.)

---

[1] *Actually, there is a close contender: "Get rid of half the words on each page, then get rid of half of what's left." But that one gets its own chapter later.*

Think of it this way:

When I'm looking at a page that doesn't make me think, all the thought balloons over my head say things like "OK, there's the ___. And that's a ___. And there's the thing that I want."

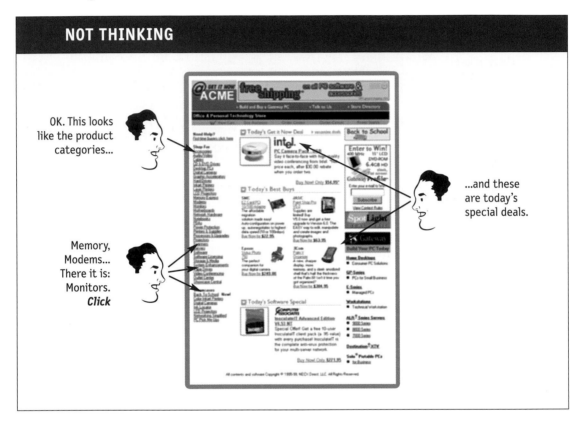

NOT THINKING

OK. This looks like the product categories...

...and these are today's special deals.

Memory, Modems... There it is: Monitors. *Click*

But when I'm looking at a page that makes me think, all the thought balloons over my head have question marks in them.

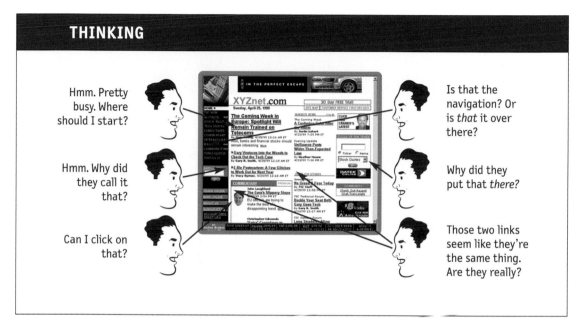

When you're creating a site, your job is to get rid of the question marks.

Things that make us think

All kinds of things on a Web page can make us stop and think unnecessarily. Take names of things, for example. Typical culprits are cute or clever names, marketing-induced names, company-specific names, and unfamiliar technical names.

For instance, suppose a friend tells me that XYZ Corp is looking to hire someone with my exact qualifications, so I head off to their Web site. As I scan the page for something to click, the name they've chosen for their job listings section makes a difference.

Note that these things are always on a continuum somewhere between "Obvious to everybody" and "Truly obscure," and there are always tradeoffs involved.

For instance, "Jobs" may sound too undignified for XYZ Corp, or they may be locked into "Job-o-Rama" because of some complicated internal politics, or because that's what it's always been called in their company newsletter. My main point is that the tradeoffs should usually be skewed further in the direction of "Obvious" than we care to think.

Another needless source of question marks over people's heads is links and buttons that aren't obviously clickable. As a user, I should never have to devote a millisecond of thought to whether things are clickable—or not.

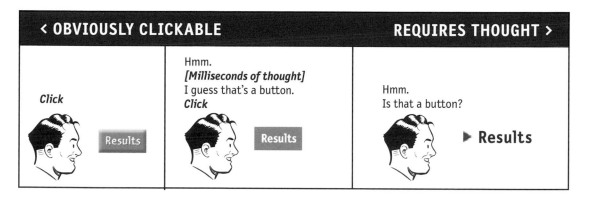

You may be thinking, "Well, it doesn't take much effort to figure out whether something's clickable. If you point the cursor at it, it'll change from an arrow to a pointing hand. What's the big deal?"

The point is, when we're using the Web every question mark adds to our cognitive workload, distracting our attention from the task at hand. The distractions may be slight but they add up, and sometimes it doesn't take much to throw us.

And as a rule, people don't *like* to puzzle over how to do things. The fact that the people who built the site didn't care enough to make things obvious—and easy—can erode our confidence in the site and its publishers.

Another example: On most bookstore sites, before I search for a book I first have to think about *how* I want to search.[2]

MOST BOOKSTORE SITES

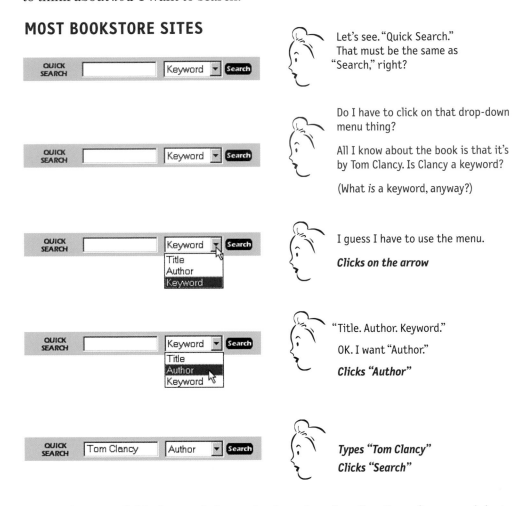

Granted, most of this "mental chatter" takes place in a fraction of a second, but you can see that it's a pretty noisy process. Even something as apparently innocent as jazzing up a well-known name (from "Search" to "Quick Search") can generate another question mark.

---

[2] *This was still true when I checked about a year ago. Only now, in 2005, have most of them finally improved.*

Amazon.com, on the other hand, doesn't even mention the Author-Title-Keyword distinction. They just look at what you type and do whatever makes the most sense.

AMAZON.COM

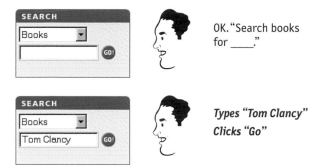

OK. "Search books for ____."

Types "Tom Clancy"
Clicks "Go"

After all, why should I have to think about *how* I want to search? And even worse, why should I have to think about how the site's search engine wants me to phrase the question, as though it were some ornery troll guarding a bridge? ("You forgot to say 'May I?'")

I could list dozens of other things that visitors to a site shouldn't spend their time thinking about, like:

> Where am I?
> Where should I begin?
> Where did they put ____?
> What are the most important things on this page?
> Why did they call it *that*?

But the last thing you need is another checklist to add to your stack of Web design checklists. The most important thing you can do is to just understand the basic principle of eliminating question marks. If you do, you'll begin to notice all the things that make *you* think while you're using the Web, and eventually you'll learn to recognize and avoid them in the pages you're building.

You can't make everything self-evident

Your goal should be for each page to be self-evident, so that just by looking at it the average user[3] will know what it is and how to use it.

Sometimes, though, particularly if you're doing something original or groundbreaking or something very complicated, you have to settle for *self-explanatory*. On a self-explanatory page, it takes a *little* thought to "get it"—but only a little. The appearance of things, their well-chosen names, the layout of the page, and the *small* amounts of carefully crafted text should all work together to create near-instantaneous recognition.

If you can't make a page self-evident, you at least need to make it self-explanatory.

Why is this so important?

Oddly enough, not for the reason you usually hear cited:

This is *sometimes* true, but you'd be surprised at how long some people will tough it out at sites that frustrate them. Many people who encounter problems with a site tend to blame themselves and not the site.

---

[3] *The actual Average User is kept in a hermetically sealed vault at the International Bureau of Standards in Geneva. We'll get around to talking about the best way to think about the "average user" eventually.*

The fact is, your site may not have been that easy to find in the first place and visitors may not know of an alternative. The prospect of starting over isn't always that attractive.

And there's also the "I've waited ten minutes for this bus already, so I may as well hang in a little longer" phenomenon. Besides, who's to say that the competition will be any less frustrating?

So why, then?

Making pages self-evident is like having good lighting in a store: it just makes everything *seem* better. Using a site that doesn't make us think about unimportant things feels effortless, whereas puzzling over things that don't matter to us tends to sap our energy and enthusiasm—and time.

But as you'll see in the next chapter when we examine how we *really* use the Web, the main reason why it's important not to make me think is that most people are going to spend far less time looking at the pages we design than we'd like to think.

As a result, if Web pages are going to be effective, they have to work most of their magic at a glance. And the best way to do this is to create pages that are self-evident, or at least self-explanatory.

How we *really* use the Web

SCANNING, SATISFICING, AND MUDDLING THROUGH

Why are things always in the last place you look for them?
Because you stop looking when you find them.

—CHILDREN'S RIDDLE

IN THE PAST TEN YEARS I'VE SPENT A LOT OF TIME WATCHING people use the Web, and the thing that has struck me most is the difference between how we think people use Web sites and how they actually use them.

When we're creating sites, we act as though people are going to pore over each page, reading our finely crafted text, figuring out how we've organized things, and weighing their options before deciding which link to click.

What they actually do most of the time (if we're lucky) is *glance* at each new page, scan *some* of the text, and click on the first link that catches their interest or vaguely resembles the thing they're looking for. There are usually large parts of the page that they don't even look at.

We're thinking "great literature" (or at least "product brochure"), while the user's reality is much closer to "billboard going by at 60 miles an hour."

WHAT WE DESIGN FOR... THE REALITY...

Read

Read

Read

Read

[Pause for reflection]

Finally, click on a carefully chosen link

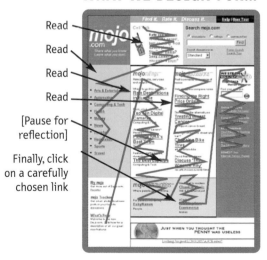

Look around feverishly for anything that

a) is interesting, or vaguely resembles what you're looking for, and

b) is clickable.

As soon as you find a halfway-decent match, click.

If it doesn't pan out, click the Back button and try again.

As you might imagine, it's a little more complicated than this, and it depends on the kind of page, what the user is trying to do, how much of a hurry she's in, and so on. But this simplistic view is much closer to reality than most of us imagine.

It makes sense that we picture a more rational, attentive user when we're designing pages. It's only natural to assume that everyone uses the Web the same way we do, and—like everyone else—we tend to think that our own behavior is much more orderly and sensible than it really is.

If you want to design effective Web pages, though, you have to learn to live with three facts about real-world Web use.

FACT OF LIFE #1:
We don't read pages. We scan them.

One of the very few well-documented facts about Web use is that people tend to spend very little time *reading* most Web pages.[1] Instead, we scan (or skim) them, looking for words or phrases that catch our eye.

The exception, of course, is pages that contain documents like news stories, reports, or product descriptions. But even then, if the document is longer than a few paragraphs, we're likely to print it out because it's easier and faster to read on paper than on a screen.

Why do we scan?

> **We're usually in a hurry.** Much of our Web use is motivated by the desire to save time. As a result, Web users tend to act like sharks: They have to keep moving, or they'll die. We just don't have the time to read any more than necessary.

> **We know we don't *need* to read everything.** On most pages, we're really only interested in a fraction of what's on the page. We're just looking for the bits that match our interests or the task at hand, and the rest of it is irrelevant. Scanning is how we find the relevant bits.

---

[1] *See Jakob Nielsen's October 1997 Alertbox column, "How Users Read on the Web" available at* www.useit.com.

> **We're good at it.** We've been scanning newspapers, magazines, and books all our lives to find the parts we're interested in, and we know that it works.

The net effect is a lot like Gary Larson's classic Far Side cartoon about the difference between what we say to dogs and what they hear. In the cartoon, the dog (named Ginger) appears to be listening intently as her owner gives her a serious talking-to about staying out of the garbage. But from the dog's point of view, all he's saying is "blah blah GINGER blah blah blah blah GINGER blah blah blah."

What we see when we look at a Web page depends on what we have in mind, but it's usually just a fraction of what's on the page.

WHAT DESIGNERS BUILD...   WHAT USERS SEE...

I want to buy a ticket.

How do I check my frequent flyer miles?

Like Ginger, we tend to focus on words and phrases that seem to match (a) the task at hand or (b) our current or ongoing personal interests. And of course, (c) the trigger words that are hardwired into our nervous systems, like "Free," Sale," and "Sex," and our own name.

FACT OF LIFE #2:
We don't make optimal choices. We satisfice.

When we're designing pages, we tend to assume that users will scan the page, consider all of the available options, and choose the best one.

In reality, though, most of the time we *don't* choose the best option—we choose the *first reasonable option*, a strategy known as satisficing.[2] As soon as we find a link that seems like it might lead to what we're looking for, there's a very good chance that we'll click it.

I'd observed this behavior for years, but its significance wasn't really clear to me until I read Gary Klein's book *Sources of Power: How People Make Decisions.*[3] Klein has spent many years studying naturalistic decision making: how people like firefighters, pilots, chessmasters, and nuclear power plant operators make high-stakes decisions in real settings with time pressure, vague goals, limited information, and changing conditions.

Klein's team of observers went into their first study (of field commanders at fire scenes) with the generally accepted model of rational decision making: Faced with a problem, a person gathers information, identifies the possible solutions, and chooses the best one. They started with the hypothesis that because of the high stakes and extreme time pressure, fire captains would be able to compare only two options, an assumption they thought was conservative.

As it turned out, the fire commanders didn't compare *any* options. They took the first reasonable plan that came to mind and did a quick mental test for problems. If they didn't find any, they had their plan of action.

---

[2] *Economist Herbert Simon coined the term (a cross between* satisfying *and* sufficing*) in* Models of Man: Social and Rational *(Wiley, 1957).*

[3] *The MIT Press, 1998.*

So why don't Web users look for the best choice?

> **We're usually in a hurry.** And as Klein points out, "Optimizing is hard, and it takes a long time. Satisficing is more efficient."

> **There's not much of a penalty for guessing wrong.** Unlike firefighting, the penalty for guessing wrong on a Web site is usually only a click or two of the Back button, making satisficing an effective strategy. (The Back button is the most-used feature of Web browsers.)

> Of course, this assumes that pages load quickly; when they don't, we have to make our choices more carefully—just one of the many reasons why most Web users don't like slow-loading pages.

> **Weighing options may not improve our chances.** On poorly designed sites, putting effort into making the best choice doesn't really help. You're usually better off going with your first guess and using the Back button if it doesn't work out.

> **Guessing is more fun.** It's less work than weighing options, and if you guess right, it's faster. And it introduces an element of chance—the pleasant possibility of running into something surprising and good.

Of course, this is not to say that users never weigh options before they click. It depends on things like their frame of mind, how pressed they are for time, and how much confidence they have in the site.

FACT OF LIFE #3:

We don't figure out how things work.
We muddle through.

One of the things that becomes obvious as soon as you do any usability testing—whether you're testing Web sites, software, or household appliances—is the extent to which people use things all the time without understanding how they work, or with completely wrong-headed ideas about how they work.

Faced with any sort of technology, very few people take the time to read instructions. Instead, we forge ahead and muddle through, making up our own vaguely plausible stories about what we're doing and why it works.

It often reminds me of the scene at the end of *The Prince and the Pauper* where the real prince discovers that the look-alike pauper has been using the Great Seal of England as a nutcracker in his absence. (It makes perfect sense—to him, the seal is just this great big, heavy chunk of metal.)

The Prince and the Pauper (Classics Illustrated)

And the fact is, we get things done that way. I've seen lots of people use software and Web sites effectively in ways that are nothing like what the designers intended.

My favorite example is the people (and I've seen at least a dozen of them myself during user tests) who will type a site's entire URL in the Yahoo search box every time they want to go there—not just to find the site for the first time, but *every time* they want to go there, sometimes several times a day. If you ask them about it, it becomes clear that some of them think that Yahoo *is* the Internet, and that this is the way you use it.[4]

Most Web designers would be shocked if they knew how many people type URLs in Yahoo's search box.

And muddling through is not limited to beginners. Even technically savvy users often have surprising gaps in their understanding of how things work. (I wouldn't be surprised if even Bill Gates has some bits of technology in his life that he uses by muddling through.)

---

[4] *In the same vein, I've encountered many AOL users who clearly think that AOL is the Internet—good news for Yahoo and AOL.*

Why does this happen?

> **It's not important to us.** For most of us, it doesn't matter to us whether we understand how things work, as long as we can use them. It's not for lack of intelligence, but for lack of caring. In the great scheme of things, it's just not important to us.[5]

> **If we find something that works, we stick to it.** Once we find something that works—no matter how badly—we tend not to look for a better way. We'll use a better way if we stumble across one, but we seldom look for one.

It's always interesting to watch Web designers and developers observe their first usability test. The first time they see a user click on something completely inappropriate, they're surprised. (For instance, when the user ignores a nice big fat "Software" button in the navigation bar, saying something like, "Well, I'm looking for software, so I guess I'd click here on 'Cheap Stuff' because cheap is always good.") The user may even find what he's looking for eventually, but by then the people watching don't know whether to be happy or not.

The second time it happens, they're yelling "Just click on 'Software'!" The third time, you can see them thinking: "Why are we even bothering?"

And it's a good question: If people manage to muddle through so much, does it really matter whether they "get it"? The answer is that it matters a great deal because while muddling through may work sometimes, it tends to be inefficient and error-prone.

---

[5] *Web developers often have a particularly hard time understanding—or even believing—that people might feel this way, since they themselves are usually keenly interested in how things work.*

On the other hand, if users "get it":

> There's a much better chance that they'll find what they're looking for, which is good for them and for you.

> There's a better chance that they'll understand the full range of what your site has to offer—not just the parts that they stumble across.

> You have a better chance of steering them to the parts of your site that you want them to see.

> They'll feel smarter and more in control when they're using your site, which will bring them back. You can get away with a site that people muddle through only until someone builds one down the street that makes them feel smart.

If life gives you lemons...

By now you may be thinking (given this less than rosy picture of the Web audience and how they use the Web), "Why don't I just get a job at the local 7-11? At least there my efforts *might* be appreciated."

So, what's a girl to do?

I think the answer is simple: If your audience is going to act like you're designing billboards, then design great billboards.

Billboard Design 101

DESIGNING PAGES FOR SCANNING, NOT READING

FACED WITH THE FACT THAT YOUR USERS ARE WHIZZING BY, there are five important things you can do to make sure they see—and understand—as much of your site as possible:

> Create a clear visual hierarchy on each page
> Take advantage of conventions
> Break pages up into clearly defined areas
> Make it obvious what's clickable
> Minimize noise.

Create a clear visual hierarchy

One of the best ways to make a page easy to grasp in a hurry is to make sure that the *appearance* of the things on the page—all of the visual cues—clearly and accurately portray the *relationships* between the things on the page: which things are related, and which things are part of other things. In other words, each page should have a clear visual hierarchy.

Pages with a clear visual hierarchy have three traits:

> **The more important something is, the more prominent it is.** For instance, the most important headings are either larger, bolder, in a distinctive color, set off by more white space, or nearer the top of the page—or some combination of the above.

> **Things that are related logically are also related visually.** For instance, you can show that things are similar by grouping them together under a heading, displaying them in a similar visual style, or putting them all in a clearly defined area.

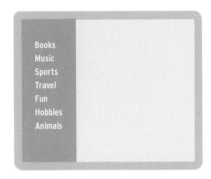

> **Things are "nested" visually to show what's part of what.** For instance, a section heading ("Computer Books") would appear above the title of a particular book, visually encompassing the whole content area of the page, because the book is part of the section. And the title in turn would span the elements that describe the book.

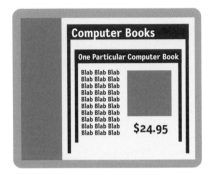

There's nothing new about visual hierarchies. Every newspaper page, for instance, uses prominence, grouping, and nesting to give us useful information about the contents of the page before we read a word. *This* picture goes with *this* story because they're both spanned by *this* headline. *This* story is the most important because it has the biggest headline, the widest column, and a prominent position on the page.

The headline spanning these three columns makes it obvious that they're all part of the same story.

The size of this headline makes it clear at a glance that this is the most important story.

We all parse visual hierarchies—online and on paper—every day, but it happens so quickly that the only time we're even vaguely aware that we're doing it is when we *can't* do it—when the visual cues (or absence of them) force us to think.

A good visual hierarchy saves us work by preprocessing the page for us, organizing and prioritizing its contents in a way that we can grasp almost instantly.

But when a page doesn't have a clear visual hierarchy—if everything looks equally important, for instance—we're reduced to the much slower process of scanning the page for revealing words and phrases, and then trying to form our own sense of what's important and how things are organized. It's a lot more work.

Besides, we want editorial guidance in Web sites, the same way we want it in other media. The publisher knows better than anyone which pieces of the site's content are most important, valuable, or popular, so why not identify them for me and save me the trouble?

Parsing a page with a visual hierarchy that's even slightly flawed—where a heading spans things that aren't part of it, for instance —is like reading a carelessly constructed sentence ("Bill put the cat on the table for a minute because it was a little wobbly.").

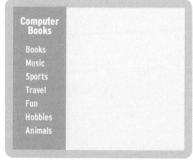

This flawed visual hierarchy suggests that all of the sections of the site are part of the Computer Books section.

Even though we can usually figure out what the sentence is supposed to mean, it still throws us momentarily and forces us to think when we shouldn't have to.

Conventions are your friends

At some point in our youth, without ever being taught, we all learned to read a newspaper. Not the words, but the conventions.

We learned, for instance, that a phrase in very large type is usually a headline that summarizes the story underneath it, and that text underneath a picture is either a caption that tells me what it's a picture *of*, or—if it's in very small type—a photo credit that tells me who took the picture.

We learned that knowing the various conventions of page layout and formatting made it easier and faster to scan a newspaper and find the stories we were interested in. And when we started traveling to other cities, we learned that all newspapers used the same conventions (with slight variations), so knowing the conventions made it easy to read *any* newspaper.

Every publishing medium develops conventions and continues to refine them and develop new ones over time.[1] The Web already has a lot of them, mostly derived from newspaper and magazine conventions, and new ones will continue to appear.

All conventions start life as somebody's bright idea. If the idea works well enough, other sites imitate it and eventually enough people have seen it in enough places that it needs no explanation. This adoption process takes time, but it happens pretty quickly on the Internet, like everything else. For instance, enough people are now familiar with the convention of using a metaphorical shopping cart on e-commerce sites that it's safe for designers to use a shopping cart icon without labeling it "Shopping cart."

---

[1] *Consider the small semitransparent logos that began appearing in the corner of your TV screen a few years ago to tell you which network you're watching. They're everywhere now, but TV had been around for 50 years before they appeared at all.*

There are two important things to know about Web conventions:

> **They're very useful.** As a
  rule, conventions only become
  conventions if they work. Well-
  applied conventions make it
  easier for users to go from site
  to site without expending a lot
  of effort figuring out how
  things work.

  There's a reassuring sense of
  familiarity, for instance, in
  seeing a list of links to the
  sections of a site on a colored
  background down the left side
  of the page, even if it's
  sometimes accompanied by a
  tedious sense of déjà vu.

Conventions
enable users to
figure out a lot
about a Web page,
even if they can't
understand a
word of it.

> **Designers are often reluctant to take advantage of them.** Faced with the
  prospect of using a convention, there's a great temptation for designers to
  reinvent the wheel instead, largely because they feel (not incorrectly) that
  they've been hired to do something new and different, and not the same old
  thing. (Not to mention the fact that praise from peers, awards, and high-profile
  job offers are rarely based on criteria like "best use of conventions.")

Sometimes time spent reinventing the wheel results in a revolutionary new rolling device. But sometimes it just amounts to time spent reinventing the wheel.

If you're not going to use an existing Web convention, you need to be sure that what you're replacing it with either (a) is so clear and self-explanatory that there's no learning curve—so it's as good as a convention, or (b) adds so much value that it's worth a small learning curve. If you're going to innovate, you have to understand the value of what you're replacing, and many designers tend to underestimate just how much value conventions provide.

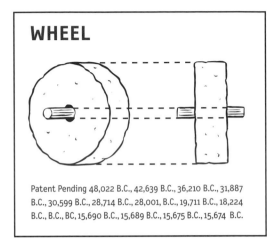

WHEEL

Patent Pending 48,022 B.C., 42,639 B.C., 36,210 B.C., 31,887 B.C., 30,599 B.C., 28,714 B.C., 28,001, B.C., 19,711 B.C., 18,224 B.C., B.C., BC, 15,690 B.C., 15,689 B.C., 15,675 B.C., 15,674 B.C.

My recommendation: Innovate when you *know* you have a better idea (and everyone you show it to says "Wow!"), but take advantage of conventions when you don't.

Break up pages into clearly defined areas

Ideally, users should be able to play a version of Dick Clark's old game show *$25,000 Pyramid* with any well-designed Web page.[2] Glancing around, they should be able to point at the different areas of the page and say, "Things I can do on this site!" "Links to today's top stories!" "Products this company sells!" "Things they're eager to sell me!" "Navigation to get to the rest of the site!"

Dividing the page into clearly defined areas is important because it allows users to decide quickly which areas of the page to focus on and which areas they can

---

[2] *Given a category like "Things a plumber uses," contestants would have to get their partners to guess the category by giving examples ("a wrench, a pipe cutter, pants that won't stay up...").*

safely ignore. Several of the initial eye-tracking studies of Web page scanning suggest that users decide very quickly which parts of the page are likely to have useful information and then almost never look at the other parts—almost as though they weren't there.

Make it obvious what's clickable

Since a large part of what people are doing on the Web is looking for the next thing to click, it's important to make it obvious what's clickable and what's not.

For example, on Senator Orrin Hatch's Home page[3] during his unsuccessful 2000 presidential bid, it wasn't clear whether everything was click-able, or nothing was. There were 18 links on the page, but only two of them invited you to click by their appearance: a large button labeled "Click here to CONTRIBUTE!" and an underlined text link ("FULL STORY").

www.orrinhatch.com

The rest of the links were colored text. But the problem was that *all* of the text on the page was in color, so there was no way to distinguish the links at a glance.

It's not a disastrous flaw. I'm sure it didn't take most users long to just start clicking on things. But when you force users to think about something that should be mindless like what's clickable, you're squandering the limited reservoir of patience and goodwill that each user brings to a new site.

---

[3] *Orrin Hatch deserves at least a footnote in usability history, since he was—to the best of my knowledge—the first presidential candidate to make Web usability a campaign issue. In the first televised Republican candidates' debate of the 2000 campaign, he told George W. Bush, "I have to say, Governor, in contrast to [your Web site], it's easy to find everything on mine. [Chuckles.] It's pretty tough to use yours! Yours is not user-friendly." (His site* was *easier to use.)*

One of my other favorite examples is the search box at drkoop.com (C. Everett Koop's health site).

Every time I use it, it makes me think, because the button that executes the search just doesn't look like a button—in spite of the fact that it has two terrific visual cues: It contains the word "**SEARCH**," which is one of the two perfect labels for a search box button,[4] and it's the only thing near the search box.

It even has a little triangular arrow graphic, which is one of the Web's conventional "Click here" indicators. But the arrow is pointing *away* from the text, as though it's pointing at something else, while the convention calls for it to be pointing *toward* the clickable text.

Moving the arrow to the left would be enough to get rid of the question mark over my head.

Keep the noise down to a dull roar

One of the great enemies of easy-to-grasp pages is visual noise. There are really two kinds of noise:

> **Busy-ness.** Some Web pages give me the same feeling I get when I'm wading through my letter from Publisher's Clearing House trying to figure out which sticker I have to attach to the form to enter without accidentally subscribing to any magazines.
>
> When everything on the page is clamoring for my attention the effect can be overwhelming: Lots of invitations to buy! Lots of exclamation points and bright colors! A lot of shouting going on!

> **Background noise.** Some pages are like being at a cocktail party; no one source of noise is loud enough to be distracting by itself, but there are a lot of tiny bits of visual noise that wear us down.

---

[4] *"Go" is the other one, but only if you also use the word "Search" as a label for the box.*

For instance, MSNBC's menus are a powerful and slick navigation device that let users get to any story in the site quickly. But the lines between items add a lot of noise. Graying the lines would make the menus much easier to scan.

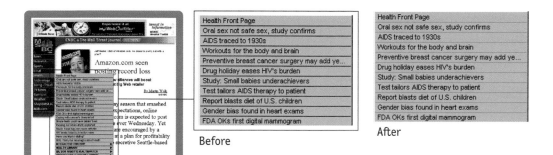

www.msnbc.com

Before

After

Users have varying tolerances for complexity and distractions; some people have no problem with busy pages and background noise, but many do. When you're designing Web pages, it's probably a good idea to assume that *everything* is visual noise until proven otherwise.

Animal, vegetable, or mineral?

WHY USERS LIKE MINDLESS CHOICES

It doesn't matter how many times I have to click, as long as
each click is a mindless, unambiguous choice.

—KRUG'S SECOND LAW OF USABILITY

WEB DESIGNERS AND USABILITY PROFESSIONALS HAVE spent a lot of time over the years debating how many times you can expect users to click to get what they want without getting too frustrated.[1] Some sites even have design rules stating that it should never take more than a specified number of clicks (usually three, four, or five) to get to any page in the site.

On the face of it, "number of clicks to get anywhere" seems like a useful criteria. But over time I've come to think that what really counts is not the number of clicks it takes me to get to what I want (although there are limits), but rather how *hard* each click is—the amount of thought required, and the amount of uncertainty about whether I'm making the right choice.

In general, I think it's safe to say that users don't mind a lot of clicks as long as each click is painless and they have continued confidence that they're on the right track—following what Jared Spool calls "the scent of information." I think the rule of thumb might be something like "three mindless, unambiguous clicks equal one click that requires thought."[2]

The classic first question in the word game Twenty Questions—"Animal, vegetable, or mineral?"—is a wonderful example of a mindless choice. As long as you accept the premise that anything that's not a plant or an animal—including things as diverse as pianos, limericks, and encyclopedias, for

---

[1] *It's actually just one part of a much broader debate about the relative merits of wide versus deep site hierarchies A wide site is broken into more categories at each level but has fewer levels, so it takes fewer clicks to get to the bottom. A deep site has more levels and requires more clicks, but there are fewer options to consider at each level.*

[2] *Of course, there are exceptions. If I'm going to have to drill down through the same parts of a site repeatedly, for instance or repeat a sequence of clicks in a Web application, or if the pages are going to take a long time to load, then the value of fewer clicks increases.*

instance—falls under "mineral," it requires no thought at all to answer the question correctly.[3]

Unfortunately, many choices on the Web aren't as clear.

For instance, if I go to Symantec's Virus Updates page because I want to update my copy of Norton AntiVirus, I'm faced with two choices I have to make before I can continue.

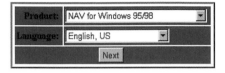

One of the choices, Language, is relatively painless. It takes only a tiny bit of thought for me to conclude that "English, US" means "United States English," as opposed to "English, UK."

If I bothered to click on the pulldown menu, though, I'd realize that I was actually just muddling through, since there is no "English, UK" on the list.

I'd also probably be a little puzzled by "Español (English, Int'l)" but I wouldn't lose any sleep over it.

The other choice, Product, is a bit dicier, however.

The problem is that it refers to "NAV for Windows 95/98." Now, I'm sure that it's perfectly clear to everyone who works at Symantec that NAV and "Norton AntiVirus" are the same, but it requires at least a small leap of faith on my part.

And even though I know for certain that I'm using Windows 98, there's at least the tiniest question in my mind whether that's exactly the same as "Windows 95/98." Maybe there *is* something called "Windows 95/98" that I just don't know about.

---

[3] *In case you've forgotten the game, there's an excellent version that you can play against on the Web at* http://www.20q.net *Created by Robin Burgener, it uses a neural net algorithm and plays a mean game. They've made it even more mindless, though, by adding "Other" and "Unknown" as acceptable answers to the first question.*

Another example: When I'm trying to buy a product or service to use in my home office, I often encounter sites that ask me to make a choice like...

> Home
> Office

Which one is me? It's the same way I feel when I'm standing in front of two mailboxes labeled Stamped Mail and Metered Mail with a business reply card in my hand. What do *they* think it is—stamped or metered? And what happens if I drop it in the wrong box?

The point is, we face choices all the time on the Web and making the choices mindless is one of the main things that make a site easy to use.

Omit ~~needless~~ words

THE ART OF NOT WRITING FOR THE WEB

O F THE FIVE OR SIX THINGS THAT I LEARNED IN college, the one that has stuck with me the longest—and benefited me the most—is E. B. White's seventeenth rule in *The Elements of Style:*

> **17. Omit needless words.**
> Vigorous writing is concise. A sentence should contain no unnecessary words, a paragraph no unnecessary sentences, for the same reason that a drawing should have no unnecessary lines and a machine no unnecessary parts.[1]

When I look at most Web pages, I'm struck by the fact that most of the words I see are just taking up space, because no one is ever going to read them. And just by being there, all the extra words suggest that you may actually *need* to read them to understand what's going on, which often makes pages seem more daunting than they actually are.

My Third Law probably sounds excessive, because it's meant to. Removing half of the words is actually a realistic goal; I find I have no trouble getting rid of half the words on most Web pages without losing anything of value. But the idea of removing half of what's left is just my way of trying to encourage people to be ruthless about it.

Getting rid of all those words that no one is going to read has several beneficial effects:

> It reduces the noise level of the page.
> It makes the useful content more prominent.
> It makes the pages shorter, allowing users to see more of each page at a glance without scrolling.

I'm not suggesting that the articles at Salon.com should be shorter than they are. I'm really talking about two specific kinds of writing: happy talk and instructions.

---

[1] *William Strunk, Jr., and E B. White,* The Elements of Style *(Allyn and Bacon, 1979).*

Happy talk must die

We all know happy talk when we see it: It's the introductory text that's supposed to welcome us to the site and tell us how great it is, or to tell us what we're about to see in the section we've just entered.

If you're not sure whether something is happy talk, there's one sure-fire test: If you listen very closely while you're reading it, you can actually hear a tiny voice in the back of your head saying, "Blah blah blah blah blah...."

A lot of happy talk is the kind of self-congratulatory promotional writing that you find in badly written brochures. Unlike good promotional copy, it conveys no useful information, and it focuses on saying how great we are, as opposed to delineating what makes us great.

Although happy talk is sometimes found on Home pages—usually in paragraphs that start with the words "Welcome to..."—its favored habitat is the front pages of the sections of a site ("section fronts"). Since these pages are often just a table of contents with no real content of their own, there's a temptation to fill them with happy talk. Unfortunately, the effect is as if a book publisher felt obligated to add a paragraph to the table of contents page saying, "This book contains many interesting chapters about ___, ___, and ___. We hope you enjoy them."

Happy talk is like small talk—content free, basically just a way to be sociable. But most Web users don't have time for small talk; they want to get right to the beef. You can—and should—eliminate as much happy talk as possible.

Instructions must die

The other major source of needless words is instructions. The main thing you need to know about instructions is that no one is going to read them—at least not until after repeated attempts at "muddling through" have failed. And even then, if the instructions are wordy, the odds of users finding the information they need is pretty low.

Your objective should always be to eliminate instructions entirely by making everything self-explanatory, or as close to it as possible. When instructions are absolutely necessary, cut them back to the bare minimum.

For example, when I click on Site Survey at the Verizon site, I get an entire screen full of instructions to read.

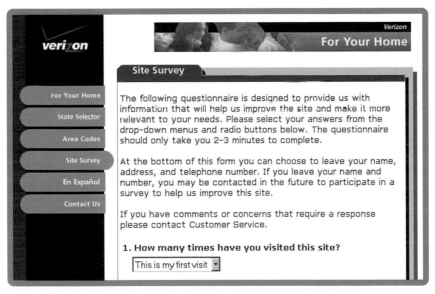

www.verizon.com

I think some aggressive pruning makes them much more useful:

BEFORE: 103 WORDS

The following questionnaire is designed to provide us with information that will help us improve the site and make it more relevant to your needs.	The first sentence is just introductory happy talk. I know what a survey is for; all I need is the words "help us" to show me that they understand that I'm doing them a favor by filling it out.
Please select your answers from the drop-down menus and radio buttons below.	Most users don't need to be told how to fill in a Web form, and the ones who do won't know what a "drop-down menu" and a "radio button" are anyway.
The questionnaire should only take you 2-3 minutes to complete.	At this point, I'm still trying to decide whether to bother with this questionnaire, so knowing that it's short is useful information.
At the bottom of this form you can choose to leave your name, address, and telephone number. If you leave your name and number, you may be contacted in the future to participate in a survey to help us improve this site.	This instruction is of no use to me at this point. It belongs at the end of the questionnaire where I can act on it. As it is, its only effect is to make the instructions look daunting.
If you have comments or concerns that require a response please contact Customer Service.	The fact that I shouldn't use this form if I want an answer is useful and important information. Unfortunately, though, they don't bother telling me *how* I contact Customer Service—or better still, giving me a link so I can do it from right here.

AFTER: 41 WORDS

Please help us improve the site by answering these questions. It should only take you 2-3 minutes to complete this survey.

NOTE: If you have comments or concerns that require a response don't use this form. Instead, please contact Customer Service.

And now for something completely different

In these first few chapters, I've been trying to convey some guiding principles that I think are good to have in mind when you're building a Web site.

Now we're heading into two chapters that look at how these principles apply to the two biggest and most important challenges in Web design: navigation and the Home page.

You might want to pack a lunch. They're very long chapters.

Street signs and Breadcrumbs

DESIGNING NAVIGATION

And you may find yourself, in a beautiful house, with a beautiful wife
And you may ask yourself, Well...How did I get here?

—TALKING HEADS, "ONCE IN A LIFETIME"

It's a fact:

People won't use your Web site if they can't find their way around it.

You know this from your own experience as a Web user. If you go to a site and can't find what you're looking for or figure out how the site is organized, you're not likely to stay long—or come back. So how do you create the proverbial "clear, simple, and consistent" navigation?

Scene from a mall

Picture this: It's Saturday afternoon and you're headed for the mall to buy a chainsaw.

As you walk through the door at Sears, you're thinking, "Hmmm. Where do they keep chainsaws?" As soon as you're inside, you start looking at the department names, high up on the walls. (They're big enough that you can read them from all the way across the store.)

TOOLS   HOUSEWARES   LAWN AND GARDEN

"Hmmm," you think, "Tools? Or Lawn and Garden?" Given that Sears is so heavily tool-oriented, you head in the direction of Tools.

When you reach the Tools department, you start looking at the signs at the end of each aisle.

POWER TOOLS   HAND TOOLS   SANDING AND GRINDING

When you think you've got the right aisle, you start looking at the individual products.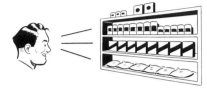

If it turns out you've guessed wrong, you try another aisle, or you may back up and start over again in the Lawn and Garden department. By the time you're done, the process looks something like this:

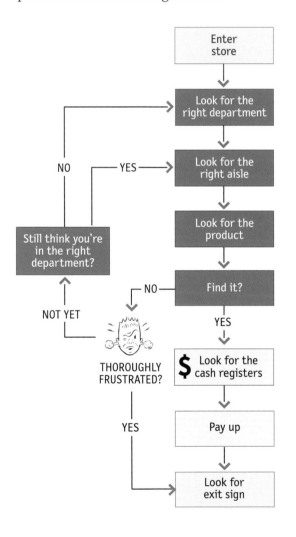

Basically, you use the store's navigation systems (the signs and the organizing hierarchy that the signs embody) and your ability to scan shelves full of products to find what you're looking for.

Of course, the actual process is a little more complex. For one thing, as you walk in the door you usually devote a few microseconds to a crucial decision: Are you going to start by looking for chainsaws on your own or are you going to ask someone where they are?

It's a decision based on a number of variables—how familiar you are with the store, how much you trust their ability to organize things sensibly, how much of a hurry you're in, and even how sociable you are.

When we factor this decision in, the process looks something like this:

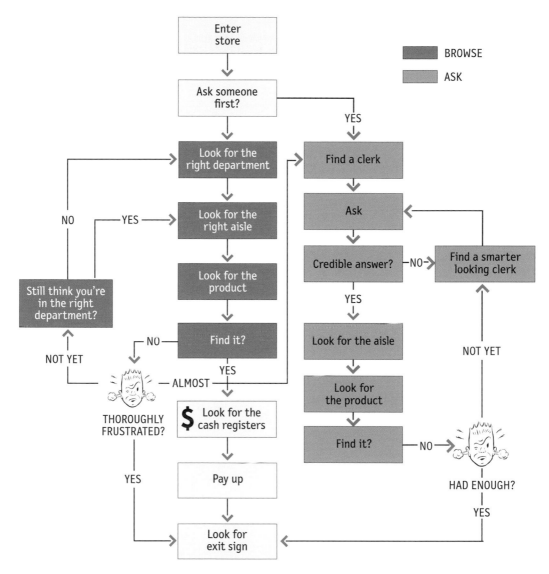

Notice that even if you start looking on your own, if things don't pan out there's a good chance that eventually you'll end up asking someone for directions anyway.

Web Navigation 101

In many ways, you go through the same process when you enter a Web site.

> **You're usually trying to find something.** In the "real" world it might be the emergency room or a can of baked beans. On the Web, it might be the cheapest 4-head VCR with Commercial Advance or the name of the actor in Casablanca who played the headwaiter at Rick's.[1]

> **You decide whether to ask first or browse first.** The difference is that on a Web site there's no one standing around who can tell you where things are. The Web equivalent of asking directions is searching—typing a description of what you're looking for in a search box and getting back a list of links to places where it *might* be.

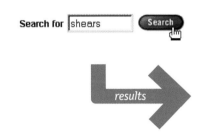
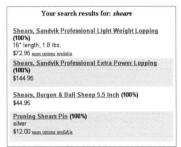

Some people (Jakob Nielsen calls them "search-dominant" users)[2] will almost always look for a search box as soon as they enter a site. (These may be the same people who look for the nearest clerk as soon as they enter a store.)

---

[1] *S. Z. "Cuddles" Sakall, born Eugene Sakall in Budapest in 1884. Ironically, most of the character actors who played the Nazi-hating denizens of Rick's Café were actually famous European stage and screen actors who landed in Hollywood after fleeing the Nazis.*

[2] *See "Search and You* May *Find" in Nielsen's archive of his Alertbox columns on* www.useit.com.

Other people (Nielsen's "link-dominant" users) will almost always browse first, searching only when they've run out of likely links to click or when they have gotten sufficiently frustrated by the site.

For everyone else, the decision whether to start by browsing or searching depends on their current frame of mind, how much of a hurry they're in, and whether the site appears to have decent browsable navigation.

> **If you choose to browse, you make your way through a hierarchy, using signs to guide you.** Typically, you'll look around on the Home page for a list of the site's main sections (like the store's department signs) and click on the one that seems right.

Then you'll choose from the list of subsections.

With any luck, after another click or two you'll end up with a list of the kind of thing you're looking for:

> 42cc Chain Saw
> 6.5hp Log Splitter
> 6.75hp Mower
> Backpack Blower
> Brushcutter
> Gas Blower/vac
> Pro 51cc Chain Saw

Then you can click on the individual links to examine them in detail, the same way you'd take products off the shelf and read the labels.

> **Eventually, if you can't find what you're looking for, you'll leave.** This is as true on a Web site as it is at Sears. You'll leave when you're convinced they haven't got it, or when you're just too frustrated to keep looking.

Here's what the process looks like:

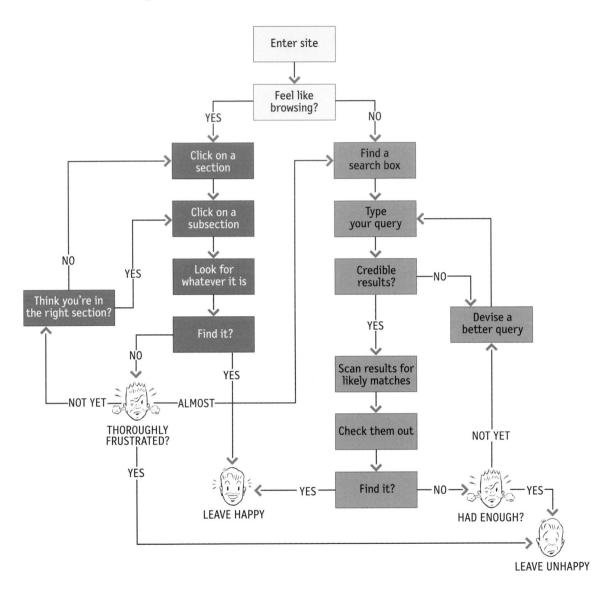

The unbearable lightness of browsing

Looking for things on a Web site and looking for them in the "real" world have a lot of similarities. When we're exploring the Web, in some ways it even *feels* like we're moving around in a physical space. Think of the words we use to describe the experience—like "cruising," "browsing," and "surfing." And clicking a link doesn't "load" or "display" another page—it "takes you to" a page.

But the Web experience is missing many of the cues we've relied on all our lives to negotiate spaces. Consider these oddities of Web space:

> **No sense of scale.** Even after we've used a Web site extensively, unless it's a very small site we tend to have very little sense of how big it is (50 pages? 1,000? 17,000?).[3] For all we know, there could be huge corners we've never explored. Compare this to a magazine, a museum, or a department store, where you always have at least a rough sense of the seen/unseen ratio.
>
> The practical result is that it's very hard to know whether you've seen everything of interest in a site, which means it's hard to know when to stop looking.[4]

> **No sense of direction.** In a Web site, there's no left and right, no up and down. We may talk about moving up and down, but we mean up and down in the hierarchy—to a more general or more specific level.

> **No sense of location.** In physical spaces, as we move around we accumulate knowledge about the space. We develop a sense of where things are and can take shortcuts to get to them.

---

[3] *Even the people who manage Web sites often have very little idea how big their sites really are.*

[4] *This is one reason why it's useful for links that we've already clicked on to display in a different color. It gives us some small sense of how much ground we've covered.*

We may get to the chainsaws the first time by following the signs, but the next time we're just as likely to think,

> "Chainsaws? Oh, yeah, I remember where they were:
> right rear corner, near the refrigerators."

And then head straight to them.

FIRST TIME   SUBSEQUENT VISITS

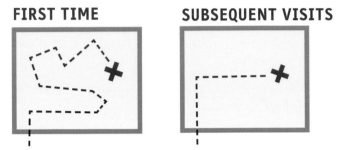

But on the Web, your feet never touch the ground; instead, you make your way around by clicking on links. Click on "Power Tools" and you're suddenly teleported to the Power Tools aisle with no traversal of space, no glancing at things along the way.

When we want to return to something on a Web site, instead of relying on a *physical* sense of where it is we have to remember where it is in the conceptual hierarchy and retrace our steps.

This is one reason why bookmarks—stored personal shortcuts—are so important, and why the Back button accounts for somewhere between 30 and 40 percent of all Web clicks.[5]

It also explains why the concept of Home pages is so important. Home pages are—comparatively—fixed places. When you're in a site, the Home page is like the North Star. Being able to click Home gives you a fresh start.

This lack of physicality is both good and bad. On the plus side, the sense of

---

[5] *L. Catledge and J. Pitkow, "Characterizing Browsing Strategies in the World-Wide Web." In* Proceedings of the Third International World Wide Web Conference, *Darmstadt, Germany (1995).*

weightlessness can be exhilarating, and partly explains why it's so easy to lose track of time on the Web—the same as when we're "lost" in a good book.[6]

On the negative side, I think it explains why we use the term "Web navigation" even though we never talk about "department store navigation" or "library navigation." If you look up *navigation* in a dictionary, it's about doing two things: getting from one place to another, and figuring out where you are.

I think we talk about Web navigation because "figuring out where you are" is a much more pervasive problem on the Web than in physical spaces. We're inherently lost when we're on the Web, and we can't peek over the aisles to see where we are. Web navigation compensates for this missing sense of place by embodying the site's hierarchy, creating a sense of "there."

Navigation isn't just a *feature* of a Web site; it *is* the Web site, in the same way that the building, the shelves, and the cash registers *are* Sears. Without it, there's no *there* there.

The moral? Web navigation had better be good.

The overlooked purposes of navigation

Two of the purposes of navigation are fairly obvious: to help us find whatever it is we're looking for, and to tell us where we are.

And we've just talked about a third:

> **It gives us something to hold on to.** As a rule, it's no fun feeling lost. (Would you rather "feel lost" or "know your way around?") Done right, navigation puts ground under our feet (even if it's virtual ground) and gives us handrails to hold on to—to make us feel grounded.

But navigation has some other equally important—and easily overlooked—functions:

> **It tells us what's here.** By making the hierarchy visible, navigation tells us what the site contains. Navigation reveals content! And revealing the site may be even more important than guiding or situating us.

---

[6] *Which may be one more reason why slow-loading pages are so bothersome: What's the fun of flying if you can only go a few miles an hour?*

> **It tells us how to use the site.** If the navigation is doing its job, it tells you *implicitly* where to begin and what your options are. Done correctly, it should be all the instructions you need. (Which is good, since most users will ignore any other instructions anyway.)

> **It gives us confidence in the people who built it.** Every moment we're in a Web site, we're keeping a mental running tally: "Do these guys know what they're doing?" It's one of the main factors we use in deciding whether to bail out and deciding whether to ever come back. Clear, well-thought-out navigation is one of the best opportunities a site has to create a good impression.

Web navigation conventions

Physical spaces like cities and buildings (and even information spaces like books and magazines) have their own navigation systems, with conventions that have evolved over time like street signs, page numbers, and chapter titles. The conventions specify (loosely) the appearance and location of the navigation elements so we know what to look for and where to look when we need them.

Putting them in a standard place lets us locate them quickly, with a minimum of effort; standardizing their appearance makes it easy to distinguish them from everything else.

For instance, we expect to find street signs at street corners, we expect to find them by looking up (not down), and we expect them to look like street signs (horizontal, not vertical).

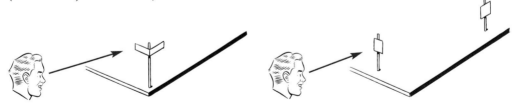

We also take it for granted that the name of a building will be above or next to its front door. In a grocery store, we expect to find signs near the ends of each aisle. In a magazine, we know there will be a table of contents somewhere in the first few pages and page numbers somewhere in the margin of each page—and that they'll look like a table of contents and page numbers.

Think of how frustrating it is when one of these conventions is broken (when magazines don't put page numbers on advertising pages, for instance).

Navigation conventions for the Web have emerged quickly, mostly adapted from existing print conventions. They'll continue to evolve, but for the moment these are the basic elements:

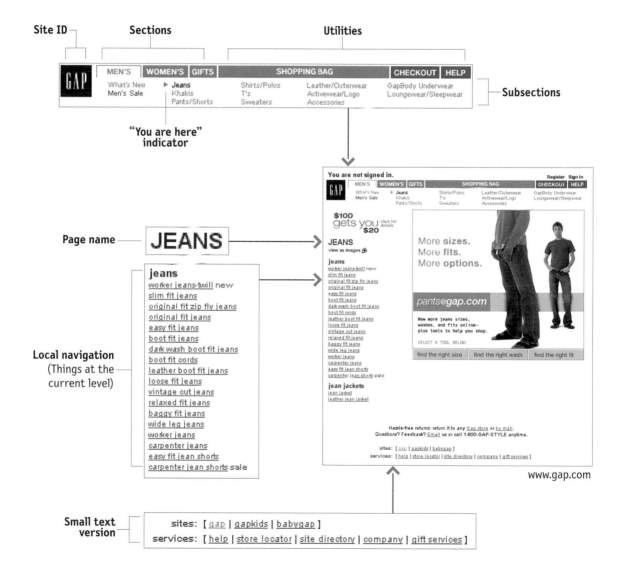

Don't look now, but I think it's following us

Web designers use the term *persistent navigation* (or *global navigation*) to describe the set of navigation elements that appear on every page of a site.

Done right, persistent navigation should say—preferably in a calm, comforting voice:

> *"The navigation is over here. Some parts will change a little*
> *depending on where you are, but it will always be here, and it*
> *will always work the same way."*

Just having the navigation appear in the same place on every page with a consistent look gives you instant confirmation that you're still in the same site—which is more important than you might think. And keeping it the same throughout the site means that (hopefully) you only have to figure out how it works once.

Persistent navigation should include the five elements you most need to have on hand at all times:

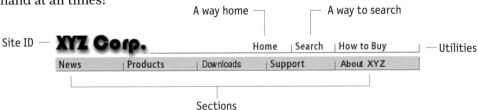

We'll look at each of them in a minute. But first...

Did I say every page?

I lied. There are two exceptions to the "follow me everywhere" rule:

> **The Home page.** The Home page is not like the other pages—it has different burdens to bear, different promises to keep. As we'll see in the next chapter, this sometimes means that it makes sense *not* to use the persistent navigation there.

> **Forms.** On pages where a form needs to be filled in, the persistent navigation can sometimes be an unnecessary distraction. For instance, when I'm paying for my purchases on an e-commerce site you don't really want me to do anything but finish filling in the forms. The same is true when I'm registering, giving feedback, or checking off personalization preferences.

> For these pages, it's useful to have a minimal version of the persistent navigation with just the Site ID, a link to Home, and any Utilities that might help me fill out the form.

Now I *know* we're not in Kansas

The Site ID or logo is like the building name for a Web site. At Sears, I really only need to see the name on my way in; once I'm inside, I *know* I'm still in Sears until I leave. But on the Web—where my primary mode of travel is teleportation—I need to see it on every page.

Ok. Now I'm in MSNBC...

Ok. I'm still in MSNBC...

...and now I'm in Planet Rx

In the same way that we expect to see the name of a building over the front entrance, we expect to see the Site ID at the top of the page—usually in (or at least near) the upper left corner.[7]

Why? Because the Site ID represents the whole site, which means it's the highest thing in the logical hierarchy of the site.

This site
Sections of this site
Subsections
Sub-subsections, etc.
This page
Areas of this page
Items on this page

And there are two ways to get this primacy across in the visual hierarchy of the page: either make it the most prominent thing on the page, or make it frame everything else.

Since you don't want the ID to be the most prominent element on the page (except, perhaps, on the Home page), the best place for it—the place that is least likely to make me think—is at the top, where it frames the entire page.

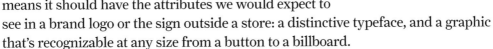

And in addition to being where we would expect it to be, the Site ID also needs to *look* like a Site ID. This means it should have the attributes we would expect to see in a brand logo or the sign outside a store: a distinctive typeface, and a graphic that's recognizable at any size from a button to a billboard.

---

[7] *...on Web pages written for left-to-right reading languages, that is. Readers of Arabic or Hebrew pages might expect the Site ID to be on the right.*

www.opus.com.il

The Sections

The Sections—sometimes called the *primary navigation*—are the links to the main sections of the site: the top level of the site's hierarchy.

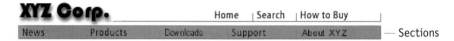 — Sections

In most cases, the persistent navigation will also include space to display the *secondary* navigation: the list of subsections in the current section.

 — Subsections

The Utilities

Utilities are the links to important elements of the site that aren't really part of the content hierarchy.

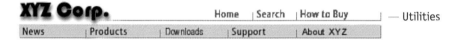 — Utilities

These are things that either can help me use the site (like Help, a Site Map, or a Shopping Cart) or can provide information about its publisher (like About Us and Contact Us).

Like the signs for the facilities in a store, the Utilities list should be slightly less prominent than the Sections.

Utilities will vary for different types of sites. For a corporate or e-commerce site, for example, they might include any of the following:

About Us	Downloads	How to Shop	Register
Archives	Directory	Jobs	Search
Checkout	Forums	My _____	Shopping Cart
Company Info	FAQs	News	Sign in
Contact Us	Help	Order Tracking	Site Map
Customer Service	Home	Press Releases	Store Locator
Discussion Boards	Investor Relations	Privacy Policy	Your Account

As a rule, the persistent navigation can accommodate only four or five Utilities— the ones users are likely to need most often. If you try to squeeze in more than that, they tend to get lost in the crowd. The less frequently used leftovers can be grouped together on the Home page.

Just click your heels three times and say, "There's no place like home."

One of the most crucial items in the persistent navigation is a button or link that takes me to the site's Home page.

Having a Home button in sight at all times offers reassurance that no matter how lost I may get, I can always start over, like pressing a Reset button or using a "Get out of Jail free" card.

There's an emerging convention that the Site ID doubles as a button that can take you to the site's Home page. It's a useful idea that every site should implement, but a surprising number of users still aren't aware of it.

For now, it's probably a good idea to either:

> include a Home page link in either the Sections or the Utilities, or

> add the word "Home" discreetly to the Site ID everywhere but the Home page to let people know that it's clickable.

Home page   Everywhere else

A way to search

Given the potential power of searching[8] and the number of people who prefer searching to browsing, unless a site is very small and very well organized, every page should have either a search box or a link to a search page. And unless there's very little reason to search your site, it should be a search box.

Keep in mind that for a large percentage of users their first official act when they reach a new site will be to scan the page for something that matches one of these three patterns:

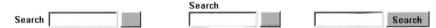

It's a simple formula: a box, a button, and the word "Search." Don't make it hard for them—stick to the formula. In particular, avoid

> **Fancy wording.** They'll be looking for the word "Search," so use the word Search, not Find, Quick Find, Quick Search, or Keyword Search. (If you use "Search" as the label for the box, use the word "Go" as the button name.)

> **Instructions.** If you stick to the formula, anyone who has used the Web for more than a few days will know what to do. Adding "Type a keyword" is like saying, "Leave a message at the beep" on your answering machine message: There was a time when it was necessary, but now it just makes you sound clueless.

---

[8] *Unfortunately, I have to say "potential" because on most sites the odds of a search producing useful results are still about 50:50. Search usability is a huge subject in itself, and the best advice I can give is to pick up a copy of* Information Architecture for the World Wide Web *by Louis Rosenfeld and Peter Morville (O'Reilly, 2002) and take to heart everything they have to say about search.*

> **Options.** If there is any possibility of confusion about the *scope* of the search (what's being searched: the site, part of the site, or the whole Web?), by all means spell it out.

But think very carefully before giving me options to limit the scope (to search just the current section of the site, for instance). And also be wary of providing options for how I specify what I'm searching for (search by title or by author, for instance, or search by part number or by product name).

I seldom see a case where the potential payoff for adding options to the persistent search box is worth the cost of making me figure out what the options are and whether I need to use them (i.e., making me think).

If you want to give me the option to scope the search, give it to me when it's useful—when I get to the search results page and discover that searching everything turned up far too many hits, so I *need* to limit the scope.

I think one of the primary reasons for Amazon's success is the robustness of its search. As I mentioned in Chapter 1, Amazon was one of the first online bookstores (if not *the* first) to drop the Title/Author/Keyword option from their search box and just take whatever I threw at them.

I've done several user tests of online bookstores, and left to their own devices, inevitably the first thing people did was search for a book they knew they should be able to find to see if the thing worked. And in test after test, the result was that people's first experience of Amazon was a successful search, while in sites that offered options many people were left puzzled when their search failed because they had misinterpreted their options.

And of course, if you're going to provide options, you need to make sure that they actually work.

For instance, when I went looking for the "Stinking badges" quote from *Treasure of the Sierra Madre* on the Internet Movie Database site, my search for "badges" using the default scope "All" found only one match—an old TV show.

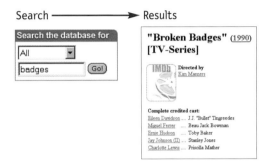

But when I changed the scope to "Quotes," there it was.

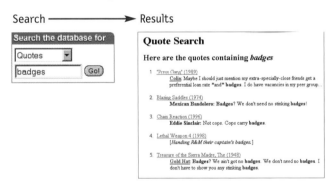

Care to take a guess what the effect was on my confidence in IMDB.com?

Secondary, tertiary, and whatever comes after tertiary

It's happened so often I've come to expect it: When designers I haven't worked with before send me preliminary page designs so I can check for usability issues, I almost inevitably get a flowchart that shows a site four levels deep...

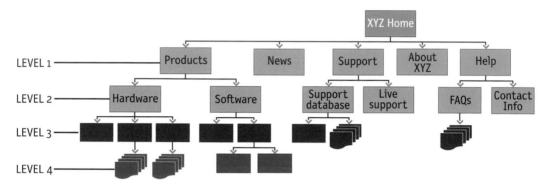

...and sample pages for the Home page and the top *two* levels.

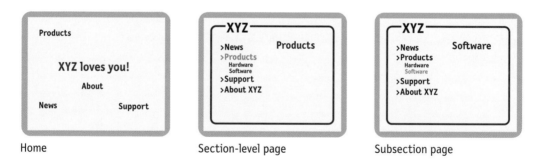

Home   Section-level page   Subsection page

I keep flipping the pages looking for more, or at least for the place where they've scrawled, "Some magic happens here," but I never find even that. I think this is one of the most common problems in Web design (especially in larger sites): failing to give the lower-level navigation the same attention as the top. In so many sites, as soon as you get past the second level, the navigation breaks down and becomes *ad hoc*. The problem is so common that it's actually hard to find good examples of third-level navigation.

Why does this happen?

Partly, I think, because good multi-level navigation is just plain hard to design—given the limited amount of space on the page, and the number of elements that have to be squeezed in.

Partly because designers usually don't even have enough time to figure out the first two levels.

Partly because it just doesn't seem that important. (After all, how important can it be? It's not primary. It's not even secondary.) And there's a tendency to think that by the time people get that far into the site, they'll understand how it works.

And then there's the problem of getting sample content and hierarchy examples for lower-level pages. Even if designers ask, they probably won't get them, because the people responsible for the content usually haven't thought things through that far, either.

But the reality is that users usually end up spending as much time on lower-level pages as they do at the top. And unless you've worked out top-to-bottom navigation from the beginning, it's very hard to graft it on later and come up with something consistent.

The moral? It's vital to have sample pages that show the navigation for all the potential levels of the site before you start arguing about the color scheme for the Home page.

Page names, or Why I love to drive in L.A.

If you've ever spent time in Los Angeles, you understand that it's not just a song lyric—L.A. really *is* a great big freeway. And because people in L.A. take driving seriously, they have the best street signs I've ever seen. In L.A.,

> Street signs are big. When you're stopped at an intersection, you can read the sign for the next cross street.

> They're in the right place—hanging *over* the street you're driving on, so all you have to do is glance up.

Now, I'll admit I'm a sucker for this kind of treatment because I come from Boston, where you consider yourself lucky if you can manage to read the street sign while there's still time to make the turn.

Los Angeles   Boston

The result? When I'm driving in L.A., I devote less energy and attention to dealing with where I am and more to traffic, conversation, and listening to *All Things Considered*. I love driving in L.A.

Page names are the street signs of the Web. Just as with street signs, when things are going well I may not notice page names at all. But as soon as I start to sense that I may not be headed in the right direction, I need to be able to spot the page name effortlessly so I can get my bearings.

There are four things you need to know about page names:

> **Every page needs a name.** Just as every corner should have a street sign, every page should have a name.

I'm at the corner of *Auctions* and *Sell an Item.*

Designers sometimes think, "Well, we've highlighted the page name in the navigation.[9] That's good enough." It's a tempting idea because it can save space, and it's one less element to work into the page layout, but it's not enough. You need a page name, too.

> **The name needs to be in the right place.** In the visual hierarchy of the page, the page name should appear to be framing the content that is unique to this page. (After all, that's what it's naming—not the navigation or the ads, which are just the infrastructure.)

---

[9] See "You are here" on page 74.

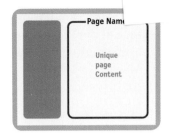

> **The name needs to be prominent.** You want the combination of position, size, color, and typeface to make the name say "This is the heading for the entire page." In most cases, it will be the largest text on the page.

> **The name needs to match what I clicked.** Even though nobody ever mentions it, every site makes an implicit social contract with its visitors:

> *The name of the page will match the words I clicked to get there.*

In other words, if I click on a link or button that says "Hot mashed potatoes," the site will take me to a page named "Hot mashed potatoes."

It may seem trivial, but it's actually a crucial agreement. Each time a site violates it, I'm forced to think, even if only for milliseconds, "Why are those two things different?" And if there's a major discrepancy between the link name and the page name or a lot of minor discrepancies, my trust in the site—and the competence of the people who publish it—will be diminished.

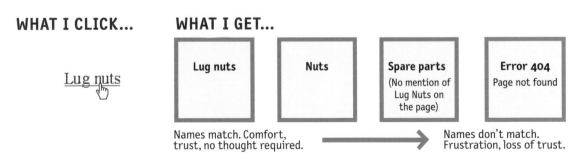

WHAT I CLICK...

Lug nuts

WHAT I GET...

Lug nuts	Nuts	Spare parts (No mention of Lug Nuts on the page)	Error 404 Page not found

Names match. Comfort, trust, no thought required. ⟶ Names don't match. Frustration, loss of trust.

Of course, sometimes you have to compromise, usually because of space limitations. If the words I click on and the page name don't match exactly, the important thing is that (a) they match as closely as possible, and (b) the reason for the difference is obvious. For instance, at Gap.com if I click the buttons labeled "Gifts for Him" and "Gifts for Her," I get pages named "gifts for men" and "gifts for women." The wording isn't identical, but they feel so equivalent that I'm not even tempted to think about the difference.

"You are here"

One of the ways navigation can counteract the Web's inherent "lost in space" feeling is by showing me where I am in the scheme of things, the same way that a "You are here" indicator does on the map in a shopping mall—or a National Park.

On the Web, this is accomplished by highlighting my current location in whatever navigational bars, lists, or menus appear on the page.

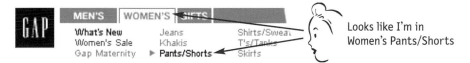

In this example, the current section (Women's) and subsection (Pants/Shorts) have both been "marked." There are a number of ways to make the current location stand out:

Put a pointer next to it	Change the text color	Use bold text	Reverse the button	Change the button color
Sports	**Sports**	Sports	**Sports**	**Sports**
Business	**Business**	Business	**Business**	**Business**
▸ **Entertainment**	Entertainment	**Entertainment**	**Entertainment**	**Entertainment**
Politics	**Politics**	Politics	**Politics**	**Politics**

The most common failing of "You are here" indicators is that they're too subtle. They need to stand out; if they don't, they lose their value as visual cues and end up just adding more noise to the page. One way to ensure that they stand out is to apply more than one visual distinction— for instance, a different color *and* bold text.

Too-subtle visual cues are actually a very common problem. Designers love subtle cues, because subtlety is one of the traits of sophisticated design. But Web users are generally in such a hurry that they routinely miss subtle cues.

In general, if you're a designer and you think a visual cue is sticking out like a sore thumb, it probably means you need to make it twice as prominent.

Breadcrumbs

Like "You are here" indicators, Breadcrumbs show you where you are. (Sometimes they even include the words "You are here.")

www.about.com

They're called Breadcrumbs because they're reminiscent of the trail of crumbs Hansel dropped in the woods so he and Gretel could find their way back home.[10]

Unlike "You are here" indicators, which show you where you are in the context of the site's hierarchy, Breadcrumbs only show you the path from the Home page to where you are.[11] (One shows you where you are in the overall scheme of things, the other shows you how to get there—kind of like the difference between looking at a road map and looking at a set of turn-by-turn directions. The directions can be very useful, but you can learn more from the map.)

You could argue that bookmarks are more like the fairy tale breadcrumbs, since we drop them as we wander, in anticipation of possibly wanting to retrace our steps someday. Or you could say that visited links (links that have changed color to show that you've clicked on them) are more like breadcrumbs since they mark the paths we've taken, and if we don't revisit them soon enough, our browser (like the birds) will swallow them up.[12]

---

[10] *In the original story, H & G's stepmother persuades their father to lose them in the forest during lean times so the whole family won't have to starve. The suspicious and resourceful H spoils the plot by dropping pebbles on the way in and following them home. But the next time(!)H is forced to use breadcrumbs instead, which prove to be a less-than-suitable substitute since birds eat them before H & G can retrace their steps. Eventually the tale devolves into attempted cannibalism, grand larceny, and immolation, but basically it's a story about how unpleasant it is to be lost.*

[11] *Actually, the truth is a little more complicated than that. If you're interested, Keith Instone has an excellent treatment of the whole subject of Breadcrumbs at* http://user-experience.org.

[12] *Visited links eventually expire and revert to their original color if you don't revisit them. The default expiration period varies from 7 to 30 days, depending on which browser you use. I*

For a long time, Breadcrumbs were an oddity, found only in sites that were really just enormous databases with very deep hierarchies, like Yahoo's Web directory...

www.yahoo.com

or grafted on to the top of very large multi-site conglomerates, like CNET...

www.cnet.com

www.gamecenter.com

www.download.com

where they managed to give users some sense of where they were in the grand scheme of things while still allowing the sub-sites to keep their independent— and often incompatible—navigation schemes.

But these days they show up in more and more sites, sometimes in lieu of well-thought-out navigation.

For most sites, I don't think that Breadcrumbs *alone* are a good navigation scheme. They're not a good replacement for showing at least the top two layers of the hierarchy, because they don't reveal enough. They give you a view, but it's like a view with blinders. It's not that you can't make your way around using just Breadcrumbs. It's that they're not a good way to *present* most sites.

Don't get me wrong. Done right, Breadcrumbs are self-explanatory, they don't take up much room, and they provide a convenient, consistent way to do two of the things you need to do most often: back up a level or go Home. It's just that I

wish I'd thought of the imaginary-birds-eating-visited-links connection myself, but Mark Bernstein first wrote about it in 1988. I came across it in Peter Glour's book Elements of Hyper-media Design, *which you can read for free online at* www.ickn.org/elements/hyper/hyper.htm.

think they're most valuable when used as part of a balanced diet, as an accessory to a solid navigational scheme, particularly for a large site with a deep hierarchy, or if you need to tie together a nest of sub-sites.

About.com has the best Breadcrumbs implementation I know of, and it illustrates several "best practices."

> **Put them at the top.** Breadcrumbs seem to work best if they're at the top of the page, above everything. I think this is probably because it literally marginalizes them—making them seem like an accessory, like page numbers in a book or magazine. When Breadcrumbs are farther down on the page they end up contending with

www.about.com

the primary navigation. Result? It makes me think. ("Which one is the real navigation? Which one should I be using?")

> **Use > between levels.** Trial and error seems to have shown that the best separator between levels is the "greater than" character (>).

www.about.com

The colon (:) and slash (/) are workable, but > seems to be the most satisfying and self-evident—probably because it visually suggests forward motion down through the levels.

> **Use tiny type**—again, to make it clear that this is just an accessory.

> **Use the words "You are here."** Most people will understand what the Breadcrumbs are, but since it's tiny type anyway it doesn't hurt to make them self-explanatory.

> **Boldface the last item.** The last item in the list should be the name of the current page, and making it bold gives it the prominence it deserves.

> **Don't use them instead of a page name.** There have been a lot of attempts to make the last item in the Breadcrumbs list do double duty, eliminating the need for a separate page name. Some sites have tried making the last item in the list the largest.

CNET : Games : Action : **Unreal Tournament**

www.gamecenter.com

This seems like it should work, but it doesn't, probably because it fights our expectation that headings are flush left or centered, not dangling in the middle of the page at the end of a list.

Four reasons why I love tabs

I haven't been able to prove it (yet), but I strongly suspect that Leonardo da Vinci invented tab dividers sometime in the late 15th century. As interface devices go, they're clearly a product of genius.[13]

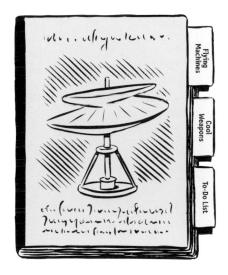

Tabs are one of the very few cases where using a physical metaphor in a user interface actually works.[14] Like the tab dividers in a three-ring binder or tabs on folders in a file drawer, they divide whatever they're sticking out of into sections. And they make it easy to open a section by reaching for its tab (or, in the case of the Web, clicking on it).

Many sites have started using tabs for navigation.

---

[13] *Memo to self: Check to see if Microsoft began using tabbed dialog boxes before Bill Gates bought the da Vinci notebook.*

[14] *The idea of dragging things to a trash can icon to delete them (conceived at Xerox PARC and popularized by Apple) is the only other one that springs to mind. And sadly, Apple couldn't resist muddying the metaphorical waters by using the same drag-to-trash action to eject diskettes—ultimately resulting in millions of identical thought balloons saying, "But wait. Won't that erase it?"*

www.catalogcity.com

www.drugstore.com

mitsloan.mit.edu

And...
800.com
Amazon.com
Beyond.com
bn.com
Borders.com
Buy.com
CDNOW
eToys.com
Fatbrain.com
Fidelity.com
LandsEnd.com
Pets.com
Quicken.com
Schwab.com
Snap.com
ToysRUs.com

I think they're an excellent navigation choice for large sites. Here's why:

> **They're self-evident.** I've never seen anyone—no matter how "computer illiterate"—look at a tabbed interface and say, "Hmmm. I wonder what *those* do?"

> **They're hard to miss.** When I do point-and-click user tests, I'm surprised at how often people can overlook button bars at the top of a Web page.[15] But because tabs are so visually distinctive, they're hard to overlook. And because they're hard to mistake for anything *but* navigation, they create the kind of obvious-at-a-glance division you want between navigation and content.

> **They're slick.** Web designers are always struggling to make pages more visually interesting. If done correctly (see below), tabs can add polish *and* serve a useful purpose.

---

[15] *I shouldn't be. I managed to use My Yahoo dozens of times before it dawned on me that the row of links at the top of the page were more sections of My Yahoo. I'd always assumed that My Yahoo was just one page and that the links were other parts of Yahoo.*

> **They suggest a physical space.** Tabs create the illusion that the active tab physically moves to the front.

It's a cheap trick, but effective, probably because it's based on a visual cue that we're very good at detecting ("things in front of other things"). Somehow, the result is a stronger-than-usual sense that the site is divided into sections and that you're *in* one of the sections.

If you love Amazon so much, why don't you marry it?

As with many other good Web practices, Amazon was one of the first sites to use tab dividers for navigation, and the first to really get them right. Over time, they tweaked and polished their implementation to the point where it was nearly perfect, even though they had to keep adding tabs as they expanded into different markets.

Eventually, they were forced to push the tab metaphor to the breaking point, but even their short-lived two-row version was remarkably well designed.

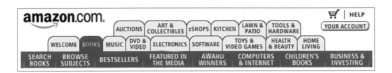

Anyone thinking of using tabs should look carefully at the design of Amazon's classic tabs, and slavishly imitate these three key attributes:

> **They were drawn correctly.** For tabs to work to full effect, the graphics have to create the visual illusion that the active tab is *in front of* the other tabs. This is the main thing that makes them feel like tabs—even more than the distinctive tab shape.[16]

To create this illusion, the active tab needs to be a different color or contrasting shade, and it has to physically connect with the space below it. This is what makes the active tab "pop" to the front.

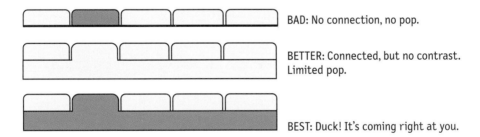

BAD: No connection, no pop.

BETTER: Connected, but no contrast. Limited pop.

BEST: Duck! It's coming right at you.

---

[16] *Whatever you do, don't use tab-shaped graphics if they're not going to behave like tabs. The Internet Movie Database—owned by Amazon, and in some ways one of the best sites on the Web—makes this mistake.*

The buttons at the top of each page look like tabs, but they act like ordinary buttons.

> **They were color coded.** Amazon used a different tab color for each section of the site, and they used the same color in the other navigational elements on the page to tie them all together.

Color coding of sections is a very good idea—as long as you don't count on everyone noticing it. Some people (roughly 1 out of 200 women and 1 out of 12 men—particularly over the age of 40) simply can't detect some color distinctions because of color-blindness.

More importantly, from what I've observed, a much larger percentage (perhaps as many as half) just aren't very *aware* of color coding in any useful way. Color is great as an additional cue, but you should never rely on it as the *only* cue.

Amazon made a point of using fairly vivid, saturated colors that are hard to miss. And since the inactive tabs were a neutral beige, there was a lot of contrast—which even color-blind users can detect—between them and the active tab.

> **There was a tab selected when you enter the site.** If there's no tab selected when I enter a site (as on Quicken.com, for instance), I lose the impact of the tabs in the crucial first few seconds, when it counts the most.

www.quicken.com

Amazon has always had a tab selected on their Home page. For a long time, it was the Books tab.

www.amazon.com

Eventually, though, as the site became increasingly less book-centric, they gave the Home page a tab of its own (labeled "Welcome").

Amazon had to create the Welcome tab so they could promote products from their other sections—not just books—on the Home page. But they did it at the risk of alienating existing customers who still think of Amazon as primarily a bookstore and hate having to click twice to get to the Books section. As usual, the interface problem is just a reflection of a deeper—and harder to solve—dilemma.

Try the trunk test

Now that you have a feeling for all of the moving parts, you're ready to try my acid test for good Web navigation. Here's how it goes:

> Imagine that you've been blindfolded and locked in the trunk of a car, then driven around for a while and dumped on a page somewhere deep in the bowels of a Web site. If the page is well designed, when your vision clears you should be able to answer these questions without hesitation:
>
> > What site is this? (Site ID)
> >
> > What page am I on? (Page name)
> >
> > What are the major sections of this site? (Sections)
> >
> > What are my options at this level? (Local navigation)
> >
> > Where am I in the scheme of things? ("You are here" indicators)
> >
> > How can I search?

Why the *Goodfellas* motif? Because it's so easy to forget that the Web experience is often more like being shanghaied than following a garden path. When you're designing pages, it's tempting to think that people will reach them by starting at the Home page and following the nice, neat paths you've laid out. But the reality is that we're often dropped down in the middle of a site with no idea where we are because we've followed a link from a search engine or from another site, and we've never seen this site's navigation scheme before.[17]

And the blindfold? You want your vision to be slightly blurry, because the true test isn't whether you can figure it out given enough time and close scrutiny. The standard needs to be that these elements pop off the page so clearly that it doesn't matter whether you're looking closely or not. You want to be relying solely on the overall appearance of things, not the details.[18]

---

[17] *This is even truer today than it was five years ago, since for many people everything they do on the Web now begins with a Google search.*

[18] *Tom Tullis of Fidelity Investments did an ingenious experiment along the same lines to evaluate the effectiveness of different page templates. He populated each template with nonsense text and asked people to identify the various elements like the page title and the site-wide navigation simply by their appearance.*

Here's how you perform the trunk test:

Step 1   Choose a page anywhere in the site at random, and print it.

Step 2   Hold it at arm's length or squint so you can't really study it closely.

Step 3   As quickly as possible, try to find and circle each item in the list below. (You won't find all of the items on every page.)

Here's one to show you how it's done.

CIRCLE: 1. Site ID

2. Page name

3. Sections and subsections

4. Local navigation

5. "You are here" indicator(s)

6. Search

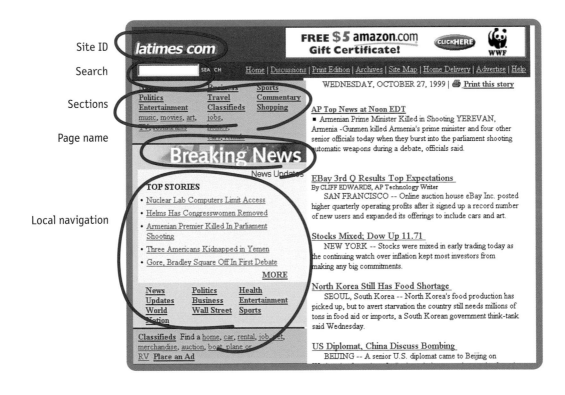

Now try it yourself on the four web pages below. Then compare your answers with mine, starting on page 90.

And when you've finished, try the same exercise on a dozen random pages from different sites. It's a great way to develop your own sense of what works and what doesn't.

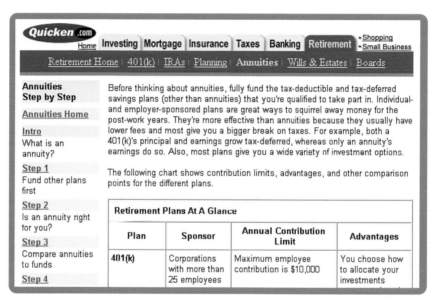

Answers on page 90

2

Answers on page 91

3

Answers on page 92

Answers on page 93

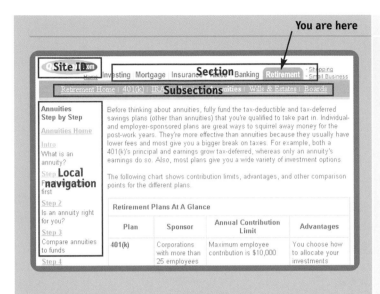

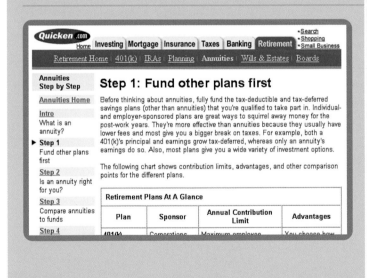

WHAT'S WRONG WITH THIS PICTURE?

"Annuities Step by Step" looks like the page name, but it's not.

The page name is actually "Fund other plans first," but you wouldn't know it because (a) there's no page name, and (b) there's no "You are here" indicator in the list on the left.

And there's no search box or search button, which is amazing for a site as large and varied (and full of useful content) as Quicken.com.

‹ MY VERSION

I've added...

> A page name at the top of the content space,

> A "You are here" indicator in the list on the left, and

> A search link, in the Utilities list.

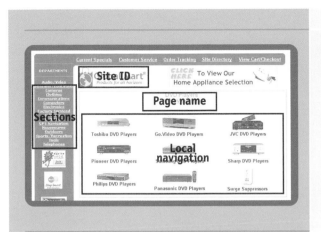

WHAT'S WRONG WITH THIS PICTURE?

The Site ID is below the navigation, and hard to spot. It looks too much like the internal promo next to it, and because the Site ID isn't in the upper left corner, it ends up looking like an ad.

The heading DVD is positioned above the link Audio/Video Main, but it is lower in the hierarchy. And there's no search, which is baffling in a large e-commerce site full of products.

< THEIR REVISED VERSION

While I was writing this chapter, Global Mart redesigned their site and did most of the right things themselves. For instance, they moved the Site ID to the top of the page and added a search box.

But as so often happens with redesigns, for every step forward there's one step back. For instance, the Utilities went from one legible line to two illegible ones. (Always avoid stacking underlined text links; they're very hard to read.)

< MY VERSION

I moved the link to Audio/Video above the page name, so the visual hierarchy matches the logical hierarchy. I also made the page name a little more prominent, and moved it flush left instead of centered. (In most cases, I find left or right alignment is more effective than centering in "telegraphing" a visual hierarchy.)

For the same reason, I moved the search button next to the search box, instead of centered below it.

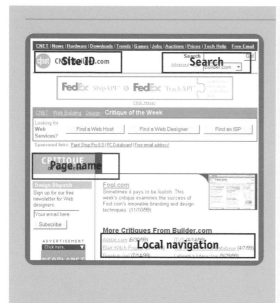

WHAT'S WRONG WITH THIS PICTURE?

The navigation is spread out all over the page, making it much harder to tell what's navigation and what isn't. The navigation, ads, promos, and content all run together.

There is no list of major sections. The list at the top looks like sections, but it's actually a list of other sub-sites of CNET.com. What makes it particularly confusing is that Builder.com (the site I'm in) doesn't appear in that list.

The only navigation that tells me where I am in Builder.com is the Breadcrumbs.

It's also hard to tell where the content actually starts. This is one of those pages that seems to keep starting over, forcing you to scroll down just to find out what it is.

‹ MY VERSION

This is one of those pages where you have to have the gumption to say, "This is beyond tweaking." There are underlying dilemmas here that need to be resolved before you even think about the page layout.

All I did was tighten up the top a little and try to make the content space easier to spot by adding a background to the column on the left.

At the same time, I made sure that the page name was positioned so it was clearly connected to the content space.

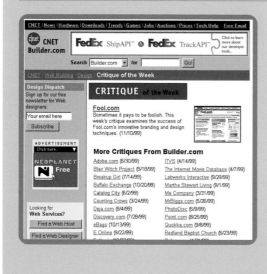

WHAT'S WRONG WITH THIS PICTURE?

Not much. Did you have trouble finding anything?

I rest my case.

< MY VERSION

There's really almost nothing to improve here.

I did redo the search. (I don't know why they used "Enter Keywords" here when they use just plain "Search" almost everywhere else in the site.)

And if you're going to scope a search, it's worth adding the word "for" so it reads like a sentence: "Search ___ for ___."

I also made the page name a little more prominent to help make the division between the content and navigation spaces even clearer.

The first step in recovery is admitting that the Home page is beyond your control

DESIGNING THE HOME PAGE

Designing a Home page often reminds me of the 50's TV game show *Beat the Clock*.

Each contestant would listen patiently while emcee Bud Collyer explained the "stunt" she had to perform. For instance, "You have 45 seconds to toss five of these water balloons into the colander strapped to your head."

The stunt always looked tricky, but doable with a little luck.

But then just as the contestant was ready to begin, Bud would always add, "Oh, there's just one more thing: you have to do it...blindfolded." Or "...under water." Or "...in the fifth dimension."

Bud Collyer offers words of encouragement to a plucky contestant

It's that way with the Home page. Just when you think you've covered all the bases, there's always just *one...more...thing*.

Think about all the things the Home page has to accommodate:

> **Site identity and mission.** Right off the bat, the Home page has to tell me what site this is and what it's for—and if possible, why I should be *here* and not at some other site.

> **Site hierarchy.** The Home page has to give an overview of what the site has to offer—both content ("What can I *find* here?") and features ("What can I *do* here?")—and how it's all organized. This is usually handled by the persistent navigation.

> **Search.** Most sites need to have a prominently displayed search box on the Home page.

> **Teases.** Like the cover of a magazine, the Home page needs to entice me with hints of the "good stuff" inside. **Content promos** spotlight the newest, best, or most popular pieces of content, like top stories and hot deals. **Feature promos** invite me to explore additional sections of the site or try out features like personalization and email newsletters.

> **Timely content.** If the site's success depends on my coming back often, the Home page probably needs to have some content that gets updated frequently. And even a site that doesn't need regular visitors needs some signs of life—even if it's only a link to a recent press release—to signal me that it's not moribund.

> **Deals.** Home page space needs to be allocated for whatever advertising, cross-promotion, and co-branding deals have been made.

> **Shortcuts.** The most frequently requested pieces of content (software updates, for instance) may deserve their own links on the Home page so people don't have to hunt for them.

> **Registration.** If the site uses registration, the Home page needs links for new users to register and for old users to sign in, and a way to let me know that I'm signed in ("Welcome back, Steve Krug").

In addition to these concrete needs, the Home page also has to meet a few abstract objectives:

> **Show me what I'm looking for.** The Home page needs to make it obvious how to get to whatever I want—assuming it's somewhere on the site.

> **...and what I'm *not* looking for.** At the same time, the Home page needs to expose me to some of the wonderful things the site has to offer that I might be interested in—even though I'm not looking for them.

> **Show me where to start.** There's nothing worse than encountering a new Home page and having no idea where to begin.

> **Establish credibility and trust.** For some visitors, the Home page will be the only chance your site gets to create a good impression.

And you have to do it...blindfolded

As if that wasn't daunting enough, it all has to be done under adverse conditions. Some of the usual constraints:

> **Everybody wants a piece of it.** Since it's the one page almost every visitor sees—and the only page some visitors will see—things that are prominently promoted on the Home page tend to get significantly greater traffic.

> As a result, the Home page is the waterfront property of the Web: It's the most desirable real estate, and there's a very limited supply. Everybody who has a stake in the site wants a promo or a link to their section on the Home page, and the turf battles for Home page visibility can be fierce.

> And given the tendency of most users to scan down the page just far enough to find an interesting link, the comparatively small amount of space "above the fold"[1] on the Home page is the *choice* waterfront property, even more fiercely fought over.

> **Too many cooks.** Because the Home page is so important, it's the one page that everybody (even the CEO) has an opinion about.

> **One size fits all.** Unlike lower-level pages, the Home page has to appeal to everyone who visits the site, no matter how diverse their interests.

---

[1] *A term inherited from newspapers, meaning the part of the page you can see without scrolling.*

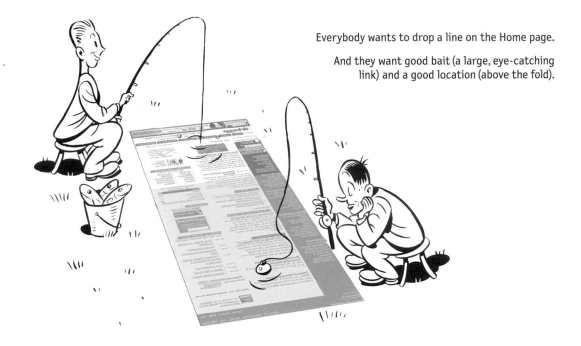

Everybody wants to drop a line on the Home page.

And they want good bait (a large, eye-catching link) and a good location (above the fold).

The First Casualty of War

Given everything the Home page has to accomplish, if a site is at all complex even the best Home page design *can't* do it all. Designing a Home page inevitably involves compromise. And as the compromises are worked out and the pressure mounts to squeeze in just one more thing, some things inevitably get lost in the shuffle.

The one thing you can't afford to lose in the shuffle—and the thing that most often gets lost—is **conveying the big picture**. Whenever someone hands me a Home page design to look at, there's one thing I can almost always count on: They haven't made it clear enough *what the site is*.

As quickly and clearly as possible, the Home page needs to answer the four questions I have in my head when I enter a new site for the first time:

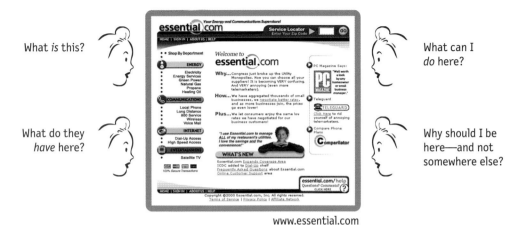

www.essential.com

I need to be able to answer these questions at a glance, correctly and unambiguously, with very little effort.

If it's not clear to me what I'm looking at in the first few seconds, interpreting everything else on the page is harder, and the chances are greater that I'll misinterpret something and get frustrated.

But if I do "get it," I'm much more likely to correctly interpret everything I see on the page, which greatly improves my chances of having a satisfying, successful experience.

Don't get me wrong: Everything else *is* important. You *do* need to impress me, entice me, direct me, and expose me to your deals. But these things won't slip through the cracks; there will always be plenty of people—inside and outside the development team—seeing to it that they get done. All too often, though, no one has a vested interest in getting the main point across.

THE TOP FIVE PLAUSIBLE EXCUSES FOR
NOT SPELLING OUT THE BIG PICTURE ON THE HOME PAGE

We don't need to. It's obvious.	When you're involved in building a site, it's so obvious to you what you're offering and why it's insanely great that it's hard to remember that it's not obvious to everybody.
After people have seen the explanation once, they will find it annoying.	Very few people will avoid a site just because they see the same explanation of what it is every time they go there—unless it takes up half the page. Think about it: Even if you know what JAMA is, will you be offended by seeing "Journal of the American Medical Association" next to the logo in small print?
Anybody who really needs our site will know what it is.	It's tempting to think that the people who don't "get" your site right away probably aren't your real audience, but it's just not true. When testing sites, it's not at all unusual to have people say, "Oh, is *that* what it is? I'd use that all the time, but it wasn't clear what it was."
That's what our advertising is for.	Even if people understood your TV, radio, and print ads,[2] by the time they get to your site will they remember exactly what it was that caught their interest?
We'll just add a "First time visitor?" link	If the site is very complex or novel, a prominent "New to this site?" link on the Home page is a good idea. But it's no substitute for spelling out the big picture in plain sight, since most people won't click on it until they've already tried—and failed—to tough it out on their own. And by then, they may already be hopelessly confused.

[2] *From the* Wall Street Journal, *March 30, 2000:*

For its debut in the 1999 Super Bowl, Outpost.com aired the now infamous ad showing "gerbils" being shot out of a cannon. [These have been replaced by] staid spots in which comedian Martin Mull explains to consumers exactly what it is Outpost.com sells (computers, technology, and electronic equipment). "We could have told you that, but we shot gerbils out of a cannon," he jokes. "What were we thinking?"

How to get the message across

Everything on the Home page can contribute to our understanding of what the site is. But there are two important places on the page where we expect to find explicit statements of what the site is about.

> **The tagline.** One of the most valuable bits of real estate is the space right next to the Site ID. When we see a phrase that's visually connected to the ID, we know it's meant to be a tagline, and so we read it as a description of the whole site. We'll look at taglines in detail in the next section.

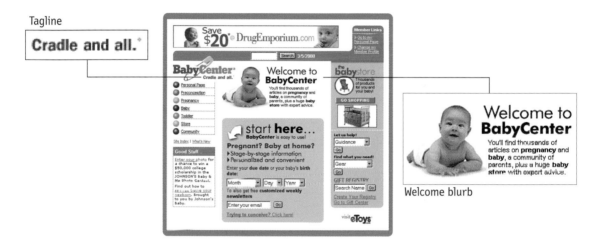

Tagline

Welcome blurb

> **The Welcome blurb.** The Welcome blurb is a terse description of the site, displayed in a prominent block on the Home page that's visible without scrolling.

The point isn't that everyone will use these two elements—or even that everyone will notice them. Most users will probably try to guess what the site is first from the overall content of the Home page. But if they can't guess, you want to have someplace on the page where they can go to find out.

There is also a third possibility: You can use the entire space to the right of the Site ID at the top of the page to expand on your mission. But if you do, you have to make sure that the visual cues make it clear that this whole area is a modifier for the Site ID and not a banner ad, since users will expect to see an ad in this space and are likely to ignore it.

Here are a few guidelines for getting the message across:

> **Use as much space as necessary.** The temptation is to not want to use *any* space because (a) you can't imagine that anybody *doesn't* know what this site is, and (b) everyone's clamoring to use the Home page space for other purposes.

Take Essential.com, for example. Because of their novel proposition (choose your own utility providers), Essential.com has a lot of 'splainin' to do, so they wisely use a lot of Home page space to do it. Almost every element on the page helps explain or reinforce what the site is about.

www.essential.com

1. Prominent tagline.

2. Prominent but terse Welcome blurb. The words Why, How, and Plus are used cleverly to make it into a bulleted list so it doesn't look like one long, imposing block of text.

3. The heading Shop By Department makes it clear that the point of these departments is to buy something, not just get information.

4. The testimonial quote (and the photo that draws your eye to it) tells the story again.

> **...but don't use any more space than necessary.** For most sites, there's no need to use a lot of space to convey the basic proposition, and messages that take up the entire Home page are usually too much for people to bother absorbing anyway. Keep it short—just long enough to get the point across, and no longer. Don't feel compelled to mention every great feature, just the most important ones (maximum four).

> **Don't use a mission statement as a Welcome blurb.** Many sites fill their Home page with their corporate mission statement that sounds like it was written by a Miss America finalist. "XYZCorp offers world-class solutions in the burgeoning field of blah blah blah blah blah...." Nobody reads them.

> **It's one of the most important things to test.** You can't trust your own judgment about this. You need to show the Home page to people from outside your organization to tell you whether the design is getting this job done because the "main point" is the one thing nobody inside the organization will notice is missing.

Nothing beats a good tagline!™

A tagline is a pithy phrase that characterizes the whole enterprise, summing up what it is and what makes it great. Taglines have been around for a long time in advertising, entertainment, and publishing: "Thousands of VCRs at impossibly low prices," "More stars than there are in the heavens,"[3] and "All the News That's Fit to Print,"[4] for example.

---

[3] *Metro-Goldwyn-Mayer studios, in the 1930's and 40's.*

[4] The New York Times. *I have to admit a personal preference for the* Mad *magazine parody version, though: "All the News That Fits, We Print."*

On a Web site, the tagline appears right below, above, or next to the Site ID.

www.alibris.com

Taglines are a very efficient way to get your message across, because they're the one place on the page where users most expect to find a concise statement of the site's purpose.

Some attributes to look for when choosing a tagline:

> Good taglines are **clear** and **informative.**

www.computerunderground.com

> Bad taglines are **vague**.

www.sonicnet.com

> Good taglines are **just long enough**. Six to eight words seem to be long enough to convey a full thought, but short enough to absorb easily.

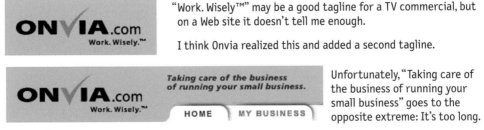

"Work. Wisely™" may be a good tagline for a TV commercial, but on a Web site it doesn't tell me enough.

I think Onvia realized this and added a second tagline.

Unfortunately, "Taking care of the business of running your small business" goes to the opposite extreme: It's too long.

www.onvia.com

> Good taglines convey **differentiation** and a **clear benefit**.

www.refdesk.com

> Bad taglines sound **generic**.

Saving time, money, and sanity are all clearly good things. But they don't tell us anything about the site.

www.netmarket.com

Don't confuse a tagline with a motto, like "We bring good things to life," "You're in good hands," or "To protect and to serve." A motto expresses a guiding principle, a goal, or an ideal, but a tagline conveys a value proposition. Mottoes are lofty and reassuring, but if I don't know what the thing is, a motto isn't going to tell me.

> Good taglines are **personable, lively,** and **sometimes clever.** Clever is good, but only if the cleverness helps convey—not obscure—the benefit.

Cradle and all" is a very clever, engaging tagline. But it might give some visitors the impression that BabyCenter.com is only about buying baby "stuff," when in reality it's also an excellent source of information and advice.

Fortunately, BabyCenter had the sense to add a prominent Welcome blurb that works: *almost* short enough to read, with a few key words in boldface to make it scannable.

www.babycenter.com

Tagline? We don't need no stinking tagline

Some sites can get by without a tagline. For instance,

> The handful of sites that have already achieved household word status.[5]

> Sites that are very well known from their offline origins.

Personally, though, I'd argue that even *these* sites would benefit from a tagline. After all, no matter how well known you are, why pass up an unobtrusive chance to tell people why they're better off at your site? And even if a site comes from a strong offline brand, the mission online is never exactly the same and it's important to explain the difference.

The fifth question

Once I know what I'm looking at, there's still one more important question that the Home page has to answer for me:

---

[5] *Even Amazon had a tagline until as late as 1998, when it was already a household word but not yet on the cover of* Time.

When I enter a new site, after a quick look around the Home page I should be able to say with confidence:

> Here's where to start if I want to search.

> Here's where to start if I want to browse.

> Here's where to start if I want to sample their best stuff.

On sites that are built around a step-by-step process (applying for a mortgage, for instance), the entry point for the process should leap out at me. And on sites where I have to register if I'm a new user or sign in if I'm a returning user, the places where I register or sign in should be prominent.

Unfortunately, the need to promote *everything* (or at least everything that supports this week's business model) sometimes obscures these entry points. It can be hard to find them when the page is full of promos yelling "Start here!" and "No, click *me* first!"

The best way to keep this from happening is to make the entry points look like entry points (i.e., make the search box look like a search box, and the list of sections look like a list of sections). It also helps to label them clearly, with labels like "Search," "Browse by Category," "Sign in," and "Start here" (for a step-by-step process).

Home page navigation can be unique

Designers sometimes ask me how important it is for the navigation on the Home page to be the same as on the rest of the site. For instance, if the persistent navigation is horizontal, can the Home page navigation be vertical?

The answer is definitely "Yes, it can be different. But not *too* different."

Given the unique responsibilities of the Home page, it often makes sense *not* to use the persistent navigation there. Typical differences include:

> **Section descriptions.** Since the Home page has to reveal as much as it can of what lies below, you may want to add a descriptive phrase to each section name, or even list the subsections—something you don't have the space to do on every page.

Home page

Everywhere else

> **Different orientation.** The Home page often requires a very different layout from all the other pages, so it may be necessary to use horizontal instead of vertical navigation, or vice versa.

> **More space for identity.** The Site ID on the Home page is usually larger than in the persistent navigation, like the large sign over a store entrance, and it usually needs some empty space next to it for the tagline, which may not appear on every page.

But it's also important not to make any changes you don't have to. The Home page navigation and the persistent navigation need to have enough in common so users can recognize immediately that they're just two different versions of the same thing.

The most important thing is to keep the section names exactly the same: the same order, the same wording, and the same grouping. It also helps to try to keep as many of the same visual cues as possible: the same typeface, colors, and capitalization.

For example, the Wildfire.com site has a very nice design and generally excellent execution, but there's too much of a disconnect between the navigation on the Home page and the rest of the site.

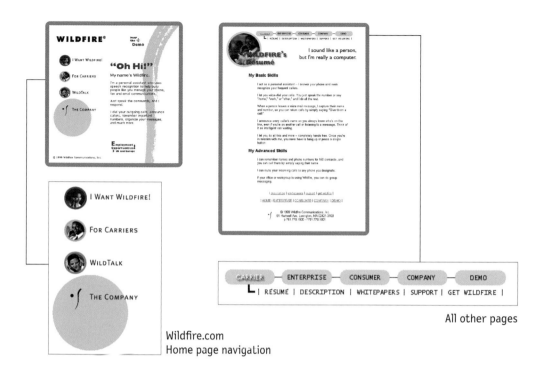

All other pages

Wildfire.com
Home page navigation

It doesn't matter that the navigation is vertical on the Home page and horizontal everywhere else. And even the minor variations in the section names (like **For Carriers** / **Carrier** and **The Company** / **Company**) are all right because it's obvious that they're the same.

What *does* matter is that once you leave the Home page

> **I Want Wildfire** becomes **Consumer**

> **WildTalk** disappears entirely

> **Enterprise** appears out of nowhere, and

> Even the names that *are* the same aren't in the same order

As a result, it's hard to recognize that the two navigation systems are related at all. When I leave the Home page, I have to figure out the site's navigation all over again, with a flurry of question marks floating over my head.

The trouble with pulldowns

Since Home page real estate is in such short supply, designers are always looking for ways to create more of it. One common approach is using pulldown menus.[6] There's no doubt about it: pulldowns definitely save space.

Pulldown menu

The same menu, displayed as a static list

Unfortunately, they suffer from several problems:

> **You have to seek them out.** You have to click on the pulldown to see the list, so there's no chance for items on the list to catch your eye as you scan the page. This can be a real drawback on the Home page where you're trying to expose the site's content.

> **They're hard to scan.** If designers use the standard HTML pulldown menu, they have no control over the font, spacing, or formatting of the list to make them more readable, and there's no really good way to divide the list into subgroups.

> **They're twitchy.** Somehow the fact that the list comes and goes so quickly makes it harder to read.

Pulldowns are most effective for alphabetized lists of items with known names, like countries, states, or products, because there's no thought involved. If I'm looking for VCRs, for instance, I can just scroll down to the V's.

But they're much less effective for lists where I don't know the name of the thing I'm looking for, especially if the list isn't alphabetized or is long enough to require scrolling.

Good   Not so good

---

[6] *...or just "pulldowns," or "drop-down menus." Nobody's quite sure what to call them.*

Unfortunately, since the main benefit of pulldowns is saving space, designers are most tempted to use them when they have a long list to display.

Some users love pulldowns because they're efficient; others won't touch them. In most cases, I think the drawbacks of pulldowns outweigh the potential benefits.

Why Golden Geese make such tempting targets, or "Funny, it tastes like chicken..."

There's something about the Home page that seems to inspire shortsighted behavior. When I sit in on meetings about Home page design, I often find the phrase "killing the golden goose" running through my head.[8]

The worst of these behaviors, of course, is the tendency to try to promote everything.

The problem with promoting things on the Home page is that it works *too* well. Anything with a prominent Home page link is guaranteed to get more traffic— usually a great deal more—leading all of the site's stakeholders to think, "Why don't I have one?"

The problem is, the rewards and the costs of adding more things to the Home page aren't shared equally. The section that's being promoted gets a huge gain in traffic, while the overall loss in effectiveness of the Home page as it gets more cluttered is shared by all sections.

---

[8] *I always thought that the phrase came from the story of Jack and the Beanstalk. In fact, Jack's Giant* did *have a goose that laid golden eggs, but nobody tried to kill it. The senseless slaughter occurs in one of Aesop's fables, and there's not much to it, plot-wise: Man finds goose, man gets greedy, man kills goose, man gets no more eggs. Moral: "Greed often overreaches itself."*

It's a perfect example of the tragedy of the commons.[9] The premise is simple: *Any shared resource (a "commons") will inevitably be destroyed by overuse.*

Take a town pasture, for example. For each animal a herdsman adds to the common pasture, he receives all proceeds from the sale of the animal—a positive benefit of +1. But the negative impact of adding an animal—its contribution to overgrazing—is shared by all, so the impact on the individual herdsman is less than –1.

The only sensible course for each herdsman is to add another animal to the herd. And another, and another—preferably before someone else does. And since each rational herdsman will reach the same conclusion, the commons is doomed.

Preserving the Home page from promotional overload requires constant vigilance, since it usually happens gradually, with the slow, inexorable addition of just...one...more...thing.

All the stakeholders need to be educated about the danger of overgrazing the Home page, and offered other methods of driving traffic, like cross-promoting from other popular pages or taking turns using the same space on the Home page.

---

[9] *The concept, originated by nineteenth-century amateur mathematician William Forster Lloyd, was popularized in a classic essay on overpopulation by biologist Garrett Hardin ("The Tragedy of the Commons,"* Science, *December 1968).*

You be the judge

Decide for yourself how well these two Home pages get the job done. Take a quick look at each one and answer these two questions, then compare your answers with mine.

> What's the point of this site?

> Do you know where to start?

Answers on page 115   www.etour.com

Answers on page 118

www.productopia.com

Each click on eTour's
"Next Site" button
opens another site.

WHAT'S THE POINT OF THIS SITE?

eTour was[10] a very interesting and (to me, at least) useful site with a simple concept: Tell them what your interests are (by checking off categories like Travel, Genealogy, or Web Design) and they'd whisk you to another hand-picked, high-quality site that matched those interests each time you clicked on their "Next Site" button.

It was effortless, rewarding Web surfing—all wheat, no chaff. I used to take eTour out for a spin every few weeks just to get a fresh sampling of what was new out there.

I think they did a very good job conveying the point of the site by reducing their story to three short phrases and numbering them 1-2-3 to suggest that using the site is a simple process.

Their tagline ("Surf the Web Without Searching") was less successful because it forced me to think about whether searching is really what makes Web surfing difficult. But as taglines go it's not bad.

Of course, eTour was luckier than most sites. Since they didn't have a content hierarchy that they have to make visible, all the Home page had to do was convey the concept and the value proposition. But even so, they did a better job than other similar sites because they stuck to the main point and resisted the temptation to tout any of the site's other features. Like any good carnival barker, they understood that the only thing that counts is getting people inside the tent.

---

[10] *eTour fell victim to Web crash in 2001, shortly after I wrote this, so I've changed it to the past tense.*

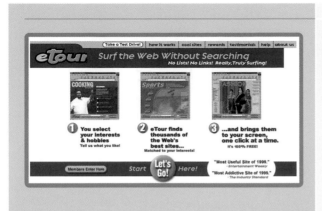

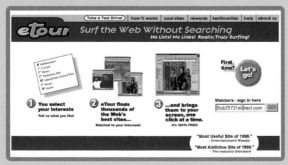

DO YOU KNOW WHERE TO START?

Most of the people I've shown eTour to were tempted to click on the numbers (1,2,3) or the three graphics first. But when that didn't work (they're not clickable), everyone clicked on the big "Let's Go!" button at the bottom of the page almost immediately.

The Big Button works well for first-time visitors. In fact, the only problem is that it's *so* big (and "Let's Go!" is so generic) that I clicked on it on my second visit, too, when what I should have clicked was the understated "Members Enter Here" button to its left. In fact, since a week or two elapsed between my subsequent visits, I clicked "Let's Go!" on my third visit, too. And my fourth.

MY VERSION

The only changes I would make would be the starting points.

I'd make it clear that the Big Button is for new users, and I'd give registered users a clear place to sign in right on the Home page.

MY VERSION #2

I always assumed that the three graphics illustrated the three steps described by the text. But when I started looking at the page carefully, I realized that they don't—they just show sample sites from three categories.

So I mocked up a version where the graphics actually did tell the story. And I was surprised to find that while it conveyed more information,

Animated GIF

it wasn't an improvement. In fact, overall it just made the concept seem more complicated. The moral? Things on a Web page don't always have to make literal sense to be effective, as long as they *seem* to make sense.

MY VERSION #3

I also tried another version where I took out the numbers (1, 2, 3), to eliminate the temptation to click on them. But I only succeeded in proving that the page works better with them. They seem to work as a sort of visual and conceptual "glue" that helps the user make sense out of the page.

The fact that users may try to click on them is a small price to pay if the numbers make the concept clear.

THEIR REDESIGN

After I first wrote this chapter, eTour redesigned their Home page. As is often the case with redesigns, they took a few steps forward...

> They created clear entry points for new and returning users by giving the Big Button a more self-explanatory name ("Sign Up") and adding a sign-in box for registered users.

> They improved the tagline ("Your Personal Web Tour Guide") and added what amounts to another tagline ("Discover Sites You'll Like, One Click at a Time").

...and a few steps back

> They combined the sign-in box with a pulldown menu, giving users one more thing to think about with very little payoff.

> They replaced the "1-2-3" graphics and text with an animated GIF and a block of text that's too long for anyone to bother reading.

WHAT'S THE POINT OF THIS SITE?

Productopia was[10] an excellent site, but you might not know it from its Home page.

The problem is a flaw in the visual hierarchy. Because the tagline ("The Source for Product Info and Advice") is tucked inside the Yahoo-style directory panel, it comes across as a description of the category list instead of the whole site. And since the tagline is bland and lacking any detail, it fails to differentiate Productopia from all the other product advice sites and ends up sounding like every other inflated Internet claim.

At first glance, the only message I get is that the site has something to do with product advice. The sophisticated graphic style and the products pictured on the left strongly suggest that we're talking about stylish, expensive products—designer furniture, not Chia Pets.

I suspect that it's a site where I could find either user reviews or reviews written by Productopia for specific products. In reality, the site is much more powerful. It offers advice on finding the best product in a category in a given price range, with actual useful advice on what makes a product good in a given category.

For instance, when I clicked on what I thought was a promo for a Dualit 2 Slice toaster, I was shocked to find myself on a page filled with useful, thoughtful, well-written information about choosing a toaster. (There was a prominent link to the Dualit, but it was only one of nine featured toasters in three categories: Quality, Style, and Value.) Overall, the Home page message gave me very little hint of what I'd find inside.

It's unclear whether the area on the left is three promos for today's featured products or a very abstract Welcome blurb. (The text, "top form / shapely showoffs smack of luxe" doesn't help much.)

---

[10] *Productopia met the same fate as eTour.*

The actual Welcome blurb statement ("Our experts provide you with the information you need...") is underneath the promos, and it needs to come before them. And, as usual, it's too long. I have to work hard to find the crucial information: editors select products without any influence from manufacturers or advertisers.

DO YOU KNOW WHERE TO START?

There are three clear starting points on the page:

> Type something in the prominent search box.

> Click on one of the categories in the Yahoo-style directory.

> Click on one of the three featured products (if that's what they are).

The only problem is, if I'm unclear on what the site *is*, how do I decide what to search for or what category to choose? A successful Home page has to tell me what the site is *and* show me where to start.

THEIR REVISED VERSION

While I was writing this chapter, Productopia redesigned their Home page, improving it substantially.

They eliminated the stray tagline on the right, and put a much better tagline ("We Help You Find the Products You'll Love") at the top of the area on the left.

And they shortened the crucial explanation ("Our experts offer unbiased advice to help you choose the product that's right for you") so that it now stands a chance of being read. But it's still buried at the bottom of what still looks like the featured products section.

And they moved the Utility links (Editorial Policy, User Reviews, and so on) into a new area at the bottom of the page, but they lumped them together with promos like "Women's Spring Fashion" and "Do You Cook?" It took me a while to figure out that the two columns were different.

MY VERSION

I'd start by moving the tagline to the top of the page with the Site ID, making it clear that it's a descriptor for the entire site.

I'd also move the Welcome blurb above the promos, and make it more prominent.

I'd separate the Utility links and the promos at the bottom of the page, grouping the promos with the "featured products" above them on the left side.

And I'd reformat the awards icons. Unlike most Web awards, these four are actually meaningful. (The Digital Time award puts Productopia on a short list of e-commerce sites with Amazon and eBay.) But lining them up across the bottom of the page makes them look like they're "Bob's Cool Site of the Day" icons. This is a case where you want to be sure you *don't* follow a convention.

"The Farmer and the Cowman Should Be Friends"

WHY MOST WEB DESIGN TEAM ARGUMENTS ABOUT USABILITY ARE A WASTE OF TIME, AND HOW TO AVOID THEM

LEFT TO THEIR OWN DEVICES, WEB DEVELOPMENT TEAMS aren't notoriously successful at making decisions about usability questions. Most teams end up spending a lot of precious time rehashing the same issues over and over.

Consider this scene:

I usually call these endless discussions "religious debates," because they have a lot in common with most discussions of religion and politics: They consist largely of people expressing strongly held personal beliefs about things that can't be proven—supposedly in the interest of agreeing on the best way to do something important (whether it's attaining eternal peace, governing effectively, or just designing Web pages). And, like most religious debates, they rarely result in anyone involved changing his or her point of view.

Besides wasting time, these arguments create tension and erode respect among team members, and can often prevent the team from making critical decisions.

Unfortunately, there are several forces at work in most Web teams that make these debates almost inevitable. In this chapter, I'll describe these forces, and explain what I think is the best antidote.

"*Everybody* likes _____."

All of us who work on Web sites have one thing in common—we're also Web *users*. And like all Web users, we tend to have strong feelings about what we like and don't like about Web sites.

As individuals, we love Flash animations because they're cool; or we hate them because they take a long time to download. We love menus down the left side of each page because they're familiar and easy to use, or we hate them because they're so boring. We really enjoy using sites with ____, or we find ____ to be a royal pain.

And when we're working on a Web team, it turns out to be very hard to check those feelings at the door.

The result is usually a room full of individuals with strong personal convictions about what makes for a good Web site.

And given the strength of these convictions—and human nature—there's a natural tendency to project these likes and dislikes onto Web users in general: to think that most Web users like the same things we like. We tend to think that most Web users are like us.

It's not that we think that *everyone* is like us. We know there are *some* people out there who hate the things we love—after all, there are even some of them on our own Web team. But not *sensible* people. And there aren't many of them.

Farmers vs. cowmen

On top of this layer of personal passion, there's another layer: professional passion. Like the farmers and the cowmen in *Oklahoma!*, the players on a Web team have very different perspectives on what constitutes good Web design based on what they do for a living.[1]

<table>
<tr><td>The ideal Web page as seen by someone whose job is...</td><td>
CEO</td><td>
Developer</td><td>
Designer</td><td>
Business development</td></tr>
</table>

Take designers and developers, for instance. Designers tend to think that most people like sites that are visually interesting because *they* like sites that are visually interesting. In fact, they probably became designers because they enjoy good design; they find that it makes things more interesting and easier to understand.[2]

Developers, on the other hand, tend to think people like sites with lots of cool features because *they* like sites with lots of cool features.

The result is that designers want to build sites that look great, and developers want to build sites with interesting, original, elegant features. I'm not sure who's the farmer and who's the cowman in this picture, but I do know that their differences in perspective often lead to conflict—and hard feelings—when it comes time to establish design priorities.

---

[1] *In the play, the thrifty, God-fearing, family-oriented farmers are always at odds with the freewheeling, loose-living cowmen. Farmers love fences, cowmen love the open range.*

[2] *Yes, I'm dealing in stereotypes here. But I think they're useful stereotypes.*

At the same time, designers and programmers find themselves siding together in another, larger clash between what Art Kleiner describes as the cultures of hype and craft.[3]

While the hype culture (upper management, marketing, and business development) is focused on making whatever promises are necessary to attract venture capital, users, strategic partners, and revenue-generating deals to the site, the burden of delivering on those promises lands on the shoulders of the craft culture artisans like the designers and programmers.

This Internet version of the perennial struggle between art and commerce (or perhaps farmers and cowmen vs. the railroad barons) adds another level of complexity to any discussions of usability issues—often in the form of apparently arbitrary edicts handed down from the hype side of the fence.[4]

---

[3] *See "Corporate Culture in Internet Time" in* strategy+business *magazine (*www.strategy-business.com/press/article/10374, *free registration required).*

[4] *I once saw a particularly puzzling feature on the Home page of a prominent—and otherwise sensibly designed—site. When I asked about it, I was told, "Oh, that. It came to our CEO in a dream, so we had to add it." True story.*

The myth of the Average User

The belief that most Web users are like us is enough to produce gridlock in the average Web design meeting. But behind that belief lies another one, even more insidious: the belief that most Web users are like *anything*.

As soon as the clash of personal and professional opinions results in a stalemate, the conversation usually turns to finding some way (whether it's an expert opinion, research, focus groups, or user tests) to determine what *most* users like or don't like—to figure out what the Average Web User is really like. The only problem is, there is no Average User.

In fact, all of the time I've spent watching people use the Web has led me to the opposite conclusion: all Web users are unique, and all Web use is basically idiosyncratic.

The more you watch users carefully and listen to them articulate their intentions, motivations, and thought processes, the more you realize that their individual reactions to Web pages are based on so many variables that attempts to describe users in terms of one-dimensional likes and dislikes are futile and counter-productive. Good design, on the other hand, takes this complexity into account.

And the worst thing about the myth of the Average User is that it reinforces the idea that good Web design is largely a matter of figuring out what people like. It's an attractive notion: either pulldowns are good (because most people like them), or they're bad (because most people don't). You should have links to everything in the site on the Home page, or you shouldn't. Menus on the top work better than menus down the side. Frames, pages that scroll, etc. are either good or bad, black or white.

The problem is there *are* no simple "right" answers for most Web design questions (at least not for the important ones). What works is good, integrated design that fills a need—carefully thought out, well executed, and tested.

Take the use of Flash, for example.[5] If asked, some percent of users will say they really like Flash, and an equal percent will probably say they hate it. But what

---

5 *Flash, Macromedia's tool for creating animated and interactive user interfaces, not flash (lowercase), the arbitrary use of whiz-bang features to make a site more interesting.*

they really hate is Flash used badly: large, complicated animations that take a long time to download and don't add any value. If you observe them carefully and ask the right questions, you'll likely find that these same people will appreciate sites that use small, hardworking, well-thought-out bits of Flash to add a pleasant bit of sizzle or useful functionality without getting in the way.

That's not to say that there aren't some things you should *never* do, and some things you should *rarely* do. There are some ways to design Web pages that are clearly wrong. It's just that they aren't the things that Web teams usually argue about.

The antidote for religious debates

The point is, it's not productive to ask questions like "Do most people like pulldown menus?" The right kind of question to ask is "Does *this* pulldown, with *these* items and *this* wording in *this* context on *this* page create a good experience for most people who are likely to use *this* site?"

And there's really only one way to answer that kind of question: testing. You have to use the collective skill, experience, creativity, and common sense of the team to build some version of the thing (even a crude version), then watch ordinary people carefully as they try to figure out what it is and how to use it.

There's no substitute for it.

Where debates about what people like waste time and drain the team's energy, testing tends to defuse arguments and break impasses by moving the discussion away from the realm of what's right or wrong and into the realm of what works or doesn't work. And by opening our eyes to just how varied users' motivations, perceptions, and responses are, testing makes it hard to keep thinking that all users are like us.

Can you tell that I think testing is a good thing?

The next chapter explains how to test your own site.

Usability testing on 10 cents a day

KEEPING TESTING SIMPLE—SO YOU DO ENOUGH OF IT

About once a month, I get one of these phone calls:

As soon as I hear "launching in two weeks" (or even "two months") and "usability testing" in the same sentence, I start to get that old fireman-headed-into-the-burning-chemical-factory feeling, because I have a pretty good idea of what's going on.

If it's two weeks, then it's almost certainly a request for a disaster check. The launch is fast approaching and everyone's getting nervous, and someone finally says, "Maybe we better do some usability testing."

If it's two months, then odds are that what they want is to settle some ongoing internal debates—usually about something very specific like color schemes. Opinion around the office is split between two different designs; some people like the sexy one, some like the elegant one. Finally someone with enough clout to authorize the expense gets tired of the arguing and says, "All right, let's get some testing done to settle this."

And while usability testing will sometimes settle these arguments, the main thing it usually ends up doing is revealing that the things they were arguing about aren't all that important. People often test to decide which color drapes are best, only to learn that they forgot to put windows in the room. For instance, they might discover that it doesn't make much difference whether you go with the horizontal navigation bar or the vertical menus if nobody understands the value proposition of your site.

Sadly, this is how most usability testing gets done: too little, too late, and for all the wrong reasons.

Repeat after me:
Focus groups are not usability tests.

Sometimes that initial phone call is even scarier:

When the last-minute request is for a focus group, it's usually a sign that the request originated in Marketing. When Web sites are being designed, the folks in Marketing often feel like they don't have much clout. Even though they're the ones who spend the most time trying to figure out who the site's audience is and what they want, the designers and developers are the ones with most of the hands-on control over how the site actually gets put together.

As the launch date approaches, the Marketing people may feel that their only hope of sanity prevailing is to appeal to a higher authority: research. And the kind of research they know is focus groups.

I often have to work very hard to make clients understand that what they need is usability testing, not focus groups. Here's the difference in a nutshell:

> In a **focus group**, a small group of people (usually 5 to 8) sit around a table and react to ideas and designs that are shown to them. It's a group process, and much of its value comes from participants reacting to each other's opinions. Focus groups are good for quickly getting a sampling of users' opinions and feelings about things.

> In a **usability test**, one user at a time is shown something (whether it's a Web site, a prototype of a site, or some sketches of individual pages) and asked to either (a) figure out what it is, or (b) try to use it to do a typical task.

Focus groups can be great for determining what your audience wants, needs, and likes—in the abstract. They're good for testing whether the idea behind the site makes sense and your value proposition is attractive. And they can be a good way to test the names you're using for features of your site, and to find out how people feel about your competitors.

But they're *not* good for learning about whether your site works and how to improve it.

The kinds of things you can learn from focus groups are the things you need to learn early on, *before* you begin designing the site. Focus groups are for EARLY in the process. You can even run them late in the process if you want to do a reality check and fine-tune your message, but *don't* mistake them for usability testing. They *won't* tell you whether people can actually use your site.

Several true things about testing

Here are the main things I know about testing:

> **If you want a great site, you've got to test**. After you've worked on a site for even a few weeks, you can't see it freshly anymore. You know too much. The only way to find out if it really works is to test it.

Testing reminds you that not everyone thinks the way you do, knows what you know, uses the Web the way you do.

I used to say that the best way to think about testing was that it was like travel: a broadening experience. It reminds you how different—and the same—people are, and gives you a fresh perspective on things.

But I finally realized that testing is really more like having friends visiting from out of town. Inevitably, as you make the tourist rounds with them, you see things about your home town that you usually don't notice because you're so used to them. And at the same time, you realize that a lot of things that you take for granted aren't obvious to everybody.

> **Testing one user is 100 percent better than testing none.** Testing always works, and even the worst test with the wrong user will show you important things you can do to improve your site. I make a point of always doing a live user test at my workshops so that people can see that it's very easy to do and it always produces an abundance of valuable insights. I ask for a volunteer and have him try to perform a task on a site belonging to one of the other attendees. These tests last less than ten minutes, but the person whose site is being tested usually scribbbles several pages of notes. And they always ask if they can have the recording of the test to show to their team back home. (One person told me that after his team saw the recording, they made one change to their site which they later calculated had resulted in $100,000 in savings.)

> **Testing one user early in the project is better than testing 50 near the end.** Most people assume that testing needs to be a big deal. But if you make it into a big deal, you won't do it early enough or often enough to get the most out of it. A simple test early—while you still have time to use what you learn from it—is almost always more valuable than a sophisticated test later.

Part of the conventional wisdom about Web development is that it's very easy to go in and make changes. The truth is, it turns out that it's not that easy to make changes to a site once it's in use. Some percentage of users will resist almost any kind of change, and even apparently simple changes often turn out to have far-reaching effects, so anything you can keep from building wrong in the first place is gravy.

> **The importance of recruiting representative users is overrated.** It's good to do your testing with people who are like the people who will use your site, but it's much more important to test early and often. My motto—as you'll see—is "Recruit loosely, and grade on a curve."

> **The point of testing is not to prove or disprove something. It's to inform your judgment.** People like to think, for instance, that they can use testing to prove whether navigation system "a" is better than navigation system "b", but you can't. No one has the resources to set up the kind of controlled experiment you'd need. What testing *can* do is provide you with invaluable input which, taken together with your experience, professional judgment, and common sense, will make it easier for you to choose wisely—and with greater confidence—between "a" and "b."

> **Testing is an iterative process.** Testing isn't something you do once. You make something, test it, fix it, and test it again.

> **Nothing beats a live audience reaction.** One reason why the Marx Brothers' movies are so wonderful is that before they started filming they would go on tour on the vaudeville circuit and perform scenes from the movie, doing five shows a day, improvising constantly and noting which lines got the best laughs. Even after they'd settled on a line, Groucho would insist on trying slight variations to see if it could be improved.

Mrs. Teasdale (Margaret Dumont) and Rufus T. Firefly eavesdrop in *Duck Soup.*

Lost our lease, going-out-of-business-sale usability testing

Usability testing has been around for a long time, and the basic idea is pretty simple: If you want to know whether your software or your Web site or your VCR remote control is easy enough to use, watch some people while they try to use it and note where they run into trouble. Then fix it, and test it again.

In the beginning, though, usability testing was a very expensive proposition. You had to have a usability lab with an observation room behind a one-way mirror, and at least two video cameras so you could record the users' reactions *and* the thing they were using. You had to recruit a lot of people so you could get results

THE TOP FIVE PLAUSIBLE EXCUSES FOR NOT TESTING WEB SITES

We don't have the time.	It's true that most Web development schedules seem to be based on the punchline from a Dilbert cartoon. If testing is going to add to everybody's to-do list, if you have to adjust development schedules around tests and involve key people in preparing for them, then it won't get done. That's why you have to make testing as small a deal as possible. Done right, it will save time, because you won't have to (a) argue endlessly, and (b) redo things at the end.
We don't have the money.	Forget $5,000 to 15,000. If you can convince someone to bring in a camcorder from home, you'll only need to spend about $300 for each round of tests.
We don't have the expertise.	The least-known fact about usability testing is that it's incredibly easy to do. Yes, some people will be better at it than others, but I've never seen a usability test fail to produce useful results, no matter how poorly it was conducted.
We don't have a usability lab.	You don't need one. All you really need is a room with a desk, a computer, and two chairs where you won't be interrupted.
We wouldn't know how to interpret the results.	One of the nicest things about usability testing is that the important lessons tend to be obvious to everyone who's watching. The serious problems are hard to miss.

that were statistically significant. It was Science. It cost $20,000 to $50,000 a shot. It didn't happen very often.

But in 1989 Jakob Nielsen wrote a paper titled "Usability Engineering at a Discount"[1] and pointed out that it didn't have to be that way. You didn't need a

---

[1] *Proceedings of the Third International Conference on Human-Computer Interaction, Boston, MA, Sept. 1989.*

usability lab, and you could achieve the same results with a lot fewer users.

The idea of discount usability testing was a huge step forward. The only problem is that a decade later most people still perceive testing as a big deal, hiring someone to conduct a test still costs $5,000 to $15,000, and as a result it doesn't happen nearly often enough.

What I'm going to commend to you in this chapter is something even more drastic: Lost our lease, going-out-of-business-sale usability testing.

I'm going to try to explain how to do your own testing when you have *no* money and *no* time. Don't get me wrong: *If you can afford to hire a professional to do your testing, by all means do it!* But *don't* do it if it means you'll do less testing.

	TRADITIONAL TESTING	LOST-OUR-LEASE TESTING
NUMBER OF USERS PER TEST	Usually eight or more to justify the set-up costs	Three or four
RECRUITING EFFORT	Select carefully to match target audience	Grab some people. Almost anybody who uses the Web will do.
WHERE TO TEST	A usability lab, with an observation room and a one-way mirror	Any office or conference room
WHO DOES THE TESTING	An experienced usability professional	Any reasonably patient human being
ADVANCE PLANNING	Tests have to be scheduled weeks in advance to reserve a usability lab and allow time for recruiting	Tests can be done almost any time, with little advance scheduling
PREPARATION	Draft, discuss, and revise a test protocol	Decide what you're going to show
WHAT/WHEN DO YOU TEST?	Unless you have a huge budget, put all your eggs in one basket and test once when the site is nearly complete	Run small tests continually throughout the development process
COST	$5,000 to $15,000 (or more)	$300 (a $50 to $100 stipend for each user) or less
WHAT HAPPENS AFTERWARDS	A 20-page written report appears a week later, then the development team meets to decide what changes to make	The development team (and interested stakeholders) debrief over lunch the same day

How many users should you test?

In most cases, I tend to think the ideal number of users for each round of testing is three, or at most four.

The first three users are very likely to encounter nearly all of the most significant problems,[2] and it's much more important to do more rounds of testing than to wring everything you can out of each round. Testing only three users helps ensure that you *will* do another round soon.[3]

Also, since you will have fixed the problems you uncovered in the first round, in the next round it's likely that all three users will uncover a new set of problems, since they won't be getting stuck on the first set of problems.

Testing only three or four users also makes it possible to test and debrief in the same day, so you can take advantage of what you've learned right away. Also, when you test more than four at a time, you usually end up with more notes than anyone has time to process—many of them about things that are really "nits," which can actually make it harder to see the forest for the trees.

In fact this is one of the reasons why I've almost completely stopped generating written reports (what I refer to as the "big honking report") for my expert reviews and for usability tests. I finally realized that for most Web teams their ability to *find* problems greatly exceeds the resources they have available to fix them, so it's important to stay focused on the most serious problems. Instead of written reports, nowadays I report my findings in a conference call with the entire Web team, which may last for an hour or two. By the end of the call, we've all agreed which problems are most important to fix, and how they're going to fix them.

---

[2] *See Jakob Nielsen's March* 2000 *Alertbox column "Why You Only Need to Test with 5 Users" at* www.useit.com *for a good discussion of the topic.*

[3] *If you're hiring someone to do the testing for you* and *money is no object, you might as well test six or eight users since the additional cost per user will be comparatively low. But* only *if it won't mean you'll do fewer rounds of testing.*

ONE TEST WITH 8 USERS

8 users

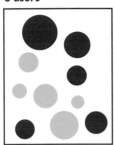

Eight users may find more problems in a single test.

But the worst problems will usually keep them from getting far enough to encounter some others.

TOTAL PROBLEMS FOUND: 5

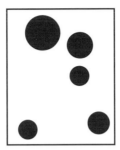

TWO TESTS WITH 3 USERS

First test: 3 users

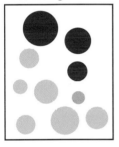

Three users may not find as many problems in a single test.

Second test: 3 users

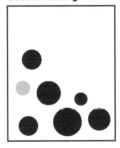

But in the second test, with the first set of problems fixed, they'll find problems they couldn't have seen in the first test.

TOTAL PROBLEMS FOUND: 9

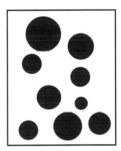

Recruit loosely and grade on a curve

When people decide to test, they often spend a lot of time trying to recruit users who they think will precisely reflect their target audience—for instance, male accountants between the ages of 25 and 30 with one to three years of computer experience who have recently purchased expensive shoes.

The best-kept secret of usability testing is the extent to which *it doesn't much matter who you test.*

For most sites, all you really need are people who have used the Web enough to know the basics.

If you can afford to hire someone to recruit the participants for you *and* it *won't* reduce the number of rounds of testing that you do, then by all means be as specific as you want. But if finding the ideal user means you're going to do fewer tests, I recommend a different approach:

Take anyone you can get (within limits) and grade on a curve.

In other words, try to find users who reflect your audience, but don't get hung up about it. Instead, try to make allowances for the differences between the people you test and your audience. I favor this approach for three reasons:

> **We're all beginners under the skin.** Scratch an expert and you'll often find someone who's muddling through—just at a higher level.

> **It's usually not a good idea to design a site so that only your target audience can use it.** If you design a site for accountants using terminology that you think all accountants will understand, what you'll probably discover is that a small but not insignificant number of accountants won't know what you're talking about. And in most cases, you need to be addressing novices as well as experts anyway, and if your grandmother can use it, an expert can.

> **Experts are rarely insulted by something that is clear enough for beginners.** Everybody appreciates clarity. (True clarity, that is, and not just something that's been "dumbed down.")

The exceptions:

> **If your site is going to be used almost exclusively by one type of user and it's no harder to recruit from that group,** then do it. For instance, if your audience will be almost entirely women, then by all means test just women.

> **If your audience is split between clearly defined groups with very divergent interests and needs,** then you need to test users from each group at least once. For instance, if you're building a university site, for at least one round of testing you want to recruit two students, two professors, two high school seniors, and two administrators. But for the other rounds, you can choose any mix.

> **If using your site requires specific domain knowledge** (e.g., a currency exchange site for money management professionals), then you need to recruit people with that domain knowledge for at least one round of tests. But don't do it for every round if it will reduce the number of tests you do.

When you're recruiting:

> **Offer a reasonable incentive.** Typical stipends for a one-hour test session range from $50 for "average" Web users to several hundred dollars for professionals from a specific domain, like cardiologists for instance. I like to offer people a little more than the going rate, since (a) it makes it clear that I value their opinion, and (b) people tend to show up on time, eager to participate. Remember, even if the session is only 30 minutes, people usually have to block out another hour for travel time. Also, I'd rather have people who are curious about the process than people who are desperate for the money.

> **Keep the invitation simple.** "We need to have a few people look at our Web site and give us some feedback. It's very easy, and would take about forty-five minutes to an hour. And you'll be paid $__ for your time."

> **Avoid discussing the site (or the organization behind the site) beforehand.** You want their first look to tell you whether they can figure out what it is from a standing start. (Of course, if they're coming to your office, they'll have a pretty good idea whose site it is.)

> **Don't be embarrassed to ask friends and neighbors.** You don't have to feel like you're imposing if you ask friends or neighbors to participate. Most people enjoy the experience. It's fun to have someone take your opinion seriously and get paid for it, and they often learn something useful that they didn't know about the Web or computers in general.

Where do you test?

All you really need is an office or conference room with two chairs, a PC or Mac (with an Internet connection, if you're testing a live site), a camcorder, a long video cable, and a tripod.

Test subject (A) sits in front of computer monitor (B), while facilitator (C) tells him what to do and asks questions. Camcorder (D) powered by squirrel (E) is pointed at the monitor to record what the subject sees.

Meanwhile, cable (F) carries signal from camcorder to TV (G) in a nearby room where interested team members (H) can observe.

You can use the video cable to run the signal from the camcorder to a TV in another office—or even a cubicle—nearby so everyone on the development team can watch without disturbing the user.

The camcorder needs to transmit what the user sees (the computer screen or the designs on paper, depending on what you're testing) and what the user and the facilitator say. In a usability lab, you'll often see a second camera used to show the observers the user's face, but this isn't necessary: The user's tone of voice usually conveys frustration pretty effectively.

You can buy the camcorder, TV, cable, and tripod for less than $600. But if your budget won't stretch that far, you can probably twist somebody's arm to bring in a camcorder from home on test days.

I don't recommend using the camcorder to videotape the sessions. In fact, I used to recommend not doing any video recording at all, because the tapes were almost never used and it made the whole process more complicated and expensive.

In the past few years though, three things have changed: PCs have gotten much faster, disk drives have gotten much larger, and screen recording software has improved dramatically. Screen recorders like Camtasia[4] run in the background on the test PC and record everything that happens on the screen and everything the user and the facilitator say in a video file you can play on the PC. It turns out that these files are very valuable because they're much easier to review quickly than videotape and they're very easy to share over a network. I recommend that you always use a screen recorder during user tests.

Who should do the testing?

Almost anyone can facilitate a usability test; all it really takes is the courage to try it. With a little practice, most people can get quite good at it.

Try to choose someone who tends to be patient, calm, empathetic, a good listener, and inherently fair. Don't choose someone whom you would describe as "definitely not a people person" or "the office crank."

Who should observe?

Anybody who wants to. It's a good idea to encourage everyone—team members, people from marketing and business development, and any other stakeholders— to attend.

When people ask me how they can convince senior management that their organization should be investing in usability, my strongest recommendation doesn't have anything to do with things like "demonstrating return on

---

[4] *There are a number of screen recorders available, but I'm partial to Camtasia, made by TechSmith, the same company that makes the screen capture program SnagIt (http://www.techsmith.com). It's very reliable and has a number of extremely useful features, and it costs about $300. For $1,000 more, they have a product called Morae specifically designed for capturing usability tests—sort of like Camtasia on steroids—which allows observers to view the test live on a networked PC, eliminating the need for a camcorder.*

investment." The tactic that I think works best is getting management to observe even one user test. Tell them that you're going to be doing some usability testing and it would be great for the Web team's morale if they could just poke their head in for a few minutes. In my experience, executives often become fascinated and stay longer than they'd planned, because it's the first time they've seen their site in action and it's often not nearly as pretty a picture as they'd imagined.

What do you test, and when do you test it?

The key is to start testing early (it's really *never* too early) and test often, at each phase of Web development.

Before you even begin designing your site, you should be testing comparable sites. They may be actual competitors, or they may be sites that are similar in style, organization, or features to what you have in mind.

Use them yourself, then watch one or two other people use them and see what works and what doesn't. Many people overlook this step, but it's invaluable—like having someone build a working prototype for you for free.

If you've never conducted a test before testing comparable sites, it will give you a pressure-free chance to get the hang of it. It will also give you a chance to develop a thick skin. The first few times you test your own site, it's hard not to take it personally when people don't get it. Testing someone else's site first will help you see how people react to sites and give you a chance to get used to it.

Since the comparable sites are "live," you can do two kinds of testing: "Get it" testing and key tasks.

> **"Get it" testing** is just what it sounds like: show them the site, and see if they get it—do they understand the purpose of the site, the value proposition, how it's organized, how it works, and so on.

> **Key task testing** means asking the user to do something, then watching how well they do.

As a rule, you'll always get more revealing results if you can find a way to observe users doing tasks that they have a hand in choosing. It's much better, for instance, to say "Find a book you want to buy, or a book you bought recently" than "Find a cookbook for under $14." When people are doing made-up tasks, they have no emotional investment in it, and they can't use as much of their personal knowledge.

As you begin designing your own site, it's never too early to start showing your design ideas to users, beginning with your first rough sketches. Designers are often reluctant to show work in progress, but users may actually feel freer to comment on something that looks unfinished, since they know you haven't got as much invested in it and it's still subject to change. Also, since it's not a polished design, users won't be distracted by details of implementation and they can focus on the essence and the wording.

Later, as you begin building parts of the site or functioning prototypes, you can begin testing key tasks on your own site.

I also recommend doing what I call Cubicle tests: Whenever you build a new kind of page—particularly forms—you should print the page out and show it to the person in the next cubicle and see if they can make sense out of it. This kind of informal testing can be very efficient, and eliminate a lot of potential problems.

A sample test session

Here's an annotated excerpt from a typical—but imaginary—test session. The site is real, but it has since been redesigned. The participant's name is Janice, and she's about 25 years old.

INTRODUCTION

Hi, Janice. My name is Steve Krug, and I'm going to be walking you through this session.

This whole first section is the script that I use when I conduct tests.[5]

You probably already know, but let me explain why we've asked you to come here today. We're testing a Web site that we're working on so we can see what it's like for actual people to use it.

I want to make it clear right away that we're testing the *site*, not you. You can't do anything wrong here. In fact, this is probably the one place today where you don't have to worry about making mistakes.

We want to hear exactly what you think, so please don't worry that you're going to hurt our feelings.[6] We want to improve it, so we need to know honestly what you think.

As we go along, I'm going to ask you to think out loud, to tell me what's going through your mind. This will help us.

I always have a copy in front of me, and I don't hesitate to read from it, but I find it's good to ad lib a little, even if it means making mistakes. When the users see that I'm comfortable making mistakes, it helps take the pressure off them.

---

[5] *A copy of the script is available on my Web site (www.sensible.com) so you can download it and edit it for your own use.*

[6] *If you didn't work on the part that's being tested, you can also say, "Don't worry about hurting my feelings. I didn't create the pages you're going to look at."*

If you have questions, just ask. I may not be able to answer them right away, since we're interested in how people do when they don't have someone sitting next to them, but I will try to answer any questions you still have when we're done.

It's important to mention this, because it will seem rude not to answer their questions as you go along. You have to make it clear before you start that (a) it's nothing personal, and (b) you'll try to answer them at the end if they still want to know.

We have a lot to do, and I'm going to try to keep us moving, but we'll try to make sure that it's fun, too.

You may have noticed the camera. With your permission, we're going to record the computer screen and what you have to say. The recording will be used only to help us figure out how to improve the site, and it won't be seen by anyone except the people working on the project. It also helps me, because I don't have to take as many notes. There are also some people watching the screen in another room.

At this point, most people will say something like, "I'm not going to end up on *America's Funniest Home Videos*, am I?"

If you would, I'm going to ask you to sign something for us. It simply says that we have your permission to record you, but that it will only be seen by the people working on the project. It also says that you won't talk to anybody about what we're showing you today, since it hasn't been made public yet.

Give them the release and non-disclosure agreement (if required) to sign. Both should be as short as possible and written in plain English.[7]

Do you have any questions before we begin?

No. I don't think so.

---

[7] *You'll find a sample recording consent form on my Web site.*

BACKGROUND QUESTIONS

Before we look at the site, I'd like to ask you just a few quick questions. First, what's your occupation?

> I'm a router.

I've never heard of that before. What does a router do, exactly?

> Not much. I take orders as they come in, and send them to the right office.

Good. Now, roughly how many hours a week would you say you spend using the Internet, including email?

> Oh, I don't know. Probably an hour a day at work, and maybe four hours a week at home. Mostly that's on the weekend. I'm too tired at night to bother. But I like playing games sometimes.

How do you spend that time? In a typical day, for instance, tell me what you do, at work and at home.

> Well, at the office I spend most of my time checking email. I get *a lot* of email, and a lot of it's junk but I have to go through it anyway. And sometimes I have to research something at work.

I find it's good to start with a few questions to get a feel for who they are and how they use the Internet. It gives them a chance to loosen up a little and gives you a chance to show that you're going to be listening attentively to what they say—and that there are no wrong or right answers.

Don't hesitate to admit your ignorance about anything. Your role here is not to come across as an expert, but as a good listener.

Notice that she's not sure how much time she really spends on the Internet. Most people aren't. Don't worry. Accurate answers aren't important here. The main point here is just to get her talking and thinking about how she uses the Internet and to give you a chance to gauge what kind of user she is.

Do you have any favorite Web sites?

> Yahoo, I guess. I like Yahoo, and I use it all
> the time. And something called
> Snakes.com, because I have a pet snake.

Really? What kind of snake?

Don't be afraid to digress
and find out a little more
about the user, as long as
you come back to the topic
before long.

> A python. He's about four feet long, but
> he should get to be eight or nine when
> he's fully grown.

Wow. OK, now, finally, have you bought
anything on the Internet? How do you feel
about buying things on the Internet?

> I've bought some things recently. I didn't
> do it for a long time, but only because I
> couldn't get things delivered. It was hard
> to get things delivered, because I'm not
> home during the day. But now one of my
> neighbors is home all the time, so I can.

And what have you bought?

> Well, I ordered a raincoat from L.L. Bean,
> and it worked out *much* better than I
> thought it would. It was actually pretty easy.

OK, great. We're done with the questions, and
we can start looking at things.

> OK, I guess.

REACTIONS TO THE HOME PAGE

First, I'm just going to ask you to look at this page and tell me what you think it is, what strikes you about it, and what you think you would click on first.

For now, don't actually click on anything. Just tell me what you *would* click on.

And again, as much as possible, it will help us if you can try to think out loud so we know what you're thinking about.

The browser has been open, but minimized. At this point, I reach over and click to maximize it.

Well, I guess the first thing I notice is that I like the color. I like the shade of orange, and I like the little picture of the sun [at the top of the page, in the eLance logo].

Let's see. [Reads.] "The global services market." "Where the world comes to get your job done."

In an average test, it's just as likely that the next user will say that she hates this shade of orange and that the drawing is too simplistic. Don't get too excited by individual reactions to site aesthetics.

I don't know what that means. I have no idea.

"Animate your logo free." [Looking at the Cool Stuff section on the left.] "3D graphics marketplace." "eLance community." "eLance marketplace."

There's a lot going on here. But I have no idea what any of it is.

If you had to take a guess, what do you think it might be?

Well, it seems to have something to do with buying and selling...something.

[Looks around the page again.] Now that I look at the list down here [the Yahoo-style category list halfway down the page], I guess maybe it must be services. Legal, financial, creative...they all sound like services.

This user is doing a good job of thinking out loud on her own. If she wasn't, this is where I'd start asking her, "What are you thinking?"

eLance Marketplaces Search the Markets ▸ [_____] GO

View all Requests for Proposals (RFPs)   More search options

Business
Consulting, Data Entry, Report
Production, Startup Services,
Transcription, Translation, Word
Processing...
RFPs | Fixed-Price

Computer
Consulting, Software Development,
Tech Support...
RFPs | Fixed-Price

Creative
Design, Illustration, Music,
Photography, Writing...

Financial
Accounting, Auditing, Bookkeeping,
Estate Planning, Insurance, Financial
Planning, Loans, Taxes...
RFPs | Fixed-Price

Legal
Claims, Corporate, Family,
Immigration, Intellectual Property,
International, Patent, Personal,
Research, Wills/Trusts...
RFPs | Fixed-Price

Marketing
Advertising, Direct...

So I guess that's what it is. Buying and selling services. Maybe like some kind of online *Yellow Pages*.

OK. Now, if you were at home, what would you click on first?

> I guess I'd click on that 3D graphics thing.
> I'm interested in 3D graphics.

Before you click on it, I have one more question. What about these pictures near the top of the page—the ones with the numbers? What did you make of them?

I ask this question because the site's designers think most users are going to start by clicking on the pictures of the five steps, and that everyone will at least look at them.

> I noticed them, but I really didn't try to figure them out. I guess I thought they were telling me what the steps in the process would be.

Any reason why you didn't pay much attention to them?

> No. I guess I just wasn't ready to start the process yet. I didn't know if I *wanted* to use it yet. I just wanted to look around first.

OK. Great.

TESTING A TASK

OK, now we're going to try something else.

Can you think of something you might want to post as a project if you were using this site?

> Hmm. Let me think. I think I saw "Home Improvement" there somewhere. We're thinking of building a deck. Maybe I would post that.

So if you were going to post the deck as a project, what would you do first?

> I guess I'd click on one of the categories down here. I think I saw home improvement. [Looks.] There it is, under "Family and Household."

So what would you do?

> Well, I'd click.... [Hesitates, looking at the two links under "Family and Household."]

Family & Household
Food & Cooking, Gardening, Genealogy, Home Improvement, Interior Design, Parenting, Pets, Real Estate...
<u>RFPs</u> | <u>Fixed-Price</u>

Now I give her a task to perform so we can see whether she can use the site for its intended purpose.

Whenever possible, it's good to let the user have some say in choosing the task.

Well, now I'm not sure *what* to do. I can't click on Home Improvement, so it looks like I have to click on either "RFPs" or "Fixed-Price." But I don't know what the difference is.

Fixed price I sort of understand; they'll give me a quote, and then they have to stick to it. But I'm not sure what RFPs is.

Well, which one do you think you'd click on?

Fixed price, I guess.

Why don't you go ahead and do it?

As it turns out, she's mistaken. Fixed-price (in this case) means services available for a fixed hourly rate, while an RFP (or Request for Proposal) is actually the choice that will elicit quotes. This is the kind of misunderstanding that often surprises the people who built the site.

From here on, I just watch while she tries to post a project, letting her continue until either (a) she finishes the task, (b) she gets really frustrated, or (c) we're not learning anything new by watching her try to muddle through.

I'd give her three or four more tasks to do, which should take not more than 45 minutes altogether.

Review the results right away

After each round of tests, you should make time as soon as possible for the development team to review everyone's observations and decide what to do next. I strongly recommend that you do three or four tests in a morning and then debrief over lunch.

You're doing two things at this meeting:

> **Triage**—reviewing the problems people saw and deciding which ones need to be fixed.
> **Problem solving**—figuring out how to fix them.

It might seem that this would be a difficult process. After all, these are the same team members who've been arguing about the right way to do things all along. So what's going to make this session any different?

Just this:

> The important things that you learn from usability testing usually *just make sense*. They tend to be obvious to anyone who watches the sessions.

Also, the experience of seeing your handiwork through someone else's eyes will often suggest entirely new solutions for problems, or let you see an old idea in a new light.

And remember, this is a cyclic process, so the team doesn't have to agree on the perfect solution. You just need to figure out what to try next.

Typical problems

Here are the types of problems you're going to see most often when you test:

> **Users are unclear on the concept.** They just don't get it. They look at the site or a page and they either don't know what to make of it, or they think they do but they're wrong.

> **The words they're looking for aren't there.** This usually means that either

(a) the categories you've used to organize your content aren't the ones they would use, or (b) the categories are what they expect, but you're just not using the names they expect.

> **There's too much going on.** Sometimes what they're looking for is right there on the page, but they're just not seeing it. In this case, you need to either (a) reduce the overall noise on the page, or (b) turn up the volume on the things they need to see so they "pop" out of the visual hierarchy more.

Some triage guidelines

Here's the best advice I can give you about deciding what to fix—and what not to.

> **Ignore "kayak" problems.** In any test, you're likely to see several cases where users will go astray momentarily but manage to get back on track almost immediately without any help. It's kind of like rolling over in a kayak; as long as the kayak rights itself quickly enough, it's all part of the so-called fun. In basketball terms, no harm, no foul.

As long as (a) everyone who has the problem notices that they're no longer headed in the right direction quickly, and (b) they manage to recover without help, and (c) it doesn't seem to faze them, you can ignore the problem. In general, if the user's second guess about where to find things is always right, that's good enough.

Of course, if there's an easy and obvious fix that won't break anything else, then by all means fix it. But kayak problems usually don't come as a surprise to the development team. They're usually there because of some ambiguity for which there is no simple resolution. For example, there are usually at least one or two oddball items that don't fit perfectly into any of the top-level categories of a site. So half the users may look for movie listings in Lifestyles first, and the other half will look for them in Arts first. Whatever you do, half of them are going to be wrong on their first guess, but everyone will get it on their second guess, which is fine.[8]

---

[8] *You may be thinking "Well, why not just put it in both categories?" In general, I think it's best for things to "live" in only one place in a hierarchy, with a prominent "see also" crosslink in any other places where people are likely to look for them.*

> **Resist the impulse to add things.** When it's obvious in testing that users aren't getting something, most people's first reaction is to add something, like an explanation or some instructions.

  Very often, the right solution is to take something (or things) away that are obscuring the meaning, rather than adding yet another distraction.

> **Take "new feature" requests with a grain of salt.** People will often say, "I'd like it better if it could do x." It always pays to be suspicious of these requests for new features. If you probe deeper, it often turns out that they already have a perfectly fine source for x and wouldn't be likely to switch; they're just telling you what they like.

> **Grab the low-hanging fruit.** The main thing you're looking for in each round of testing is the big, cheap wins. These fall into two categories:

  > **Head slappers.** These are the surprises that show up during testing where the problem and the solution were obvious to everyone the moment they saw the first user try to muddle through. These are like found money, and you should fix them right away.

  > **Cheap hits.** Also try to implement any changes that (a) require almost no effort, or (b) require a *little* effort but are highly visible.

And finally, there's one last piece of advice about "making changes" that deserves its own section:

Don't throw the baby out with the dishes

Like any good design, successful Web pages are usually a delicate balance, and it's important to keep in mind that even a minor change can have a major impact. Sometimes the real challenge isn't fixing the problems you find—it's fixing them *without* breaking the parts that already work.

Whenever you're making a change, think carefully about what else is going to be affected. In particular, when you're making something more prominent than it was, consider what else might end up being de-emphasized as a result.

One morning a month: that's all we ask

Ideally, I think every Web development team should spend one morning a month doing usability testing.

In a morning, you can test three or four users, then debrief over lunch. That's it.

When you leave lunch, the team will have decided what you're going to fix, and you'll be done with testing for the month. No reports, no endless meetings.

Doing it all in a morning also greatly increases the chances that most team members will make time to come and watch at least some of the sessions, which is highly desirable.

If you're going to try doing some testing yourself—and I hope you will—you'll find some more advice about how to do it in a chapter called "Usability testing: The Movie" that was in the first edition of this book.[9] My next book is going to be all about do-it-yourself usability testing, but I do *not* want you to wait for it before you start testing. Start now.

---

[9] *You can download the chapter for free at* http://www.sensible.com/secondedition.

Usability as common courtesy

WHY YOUR WEB SITE SHOULD BE A MENSCH[1]

---

[1] **Mensch:** *a German-derived Yiddish word originally meaning "human being." A person of integrity and honor; "a stand-up guy"; someone who does the right thing.*

Sincerity: that's the hard part.
If you can fake that, the rest is easy.

—OLD JOKE ABOUT A HOLLYWOOD AGENT

SOME TIME AGO, I WAS BOOKED ON A FLIGHT TO DENVER. AS IT happened, the date of my flight also turned out to be the deadline for collective bargaining between the airline I was booked on and one of its unions.

Concerned, I did what anyone would do: (a) Start checking Google News every hour to see if a deal had been reached, and (b) visit the airline's Web site to see what *they* were saying about it.

I was shocked to discover that not only was there nothing about the impending strike on the airline's Home page, but there wasn't a word about it to be found anywhere on the entire site. I searched. I browsed. I scrolled through all of their FAQ lists. Nothing but business as usual. "Strike? What strike?"

Now, on the morning of a potential airline strike, you have to know that there's really only one frequently asked question related to the site, and it's being asked by hundreds of thousands of people who hold tickets for the coming week: What's going to happen to me?

I might have expected to find an entire FAQ list dedicated to the topic:

> Is there really going to be a strike?
> What's the current status of the talks?
> If there is a strike, what will happen?
> How will I be able to rebook my flight?
> What will you do to help me?

Nothing.

What was I to take away from this?

Either (a) the airline had no procedure for updating their Home page for special circumstances, (b) for some legal or business reason they didn't want to admit that there might be a strike, (c) it hadn't occurred to them that people might be interested, or (d) they just couldn't be bothered.

No matter what the real reason was, they did an outstanding job of depleting my goodwill towards both the airline and their Web site. Their brand—which they spend hundreds of millions of dollars a year polishing—had definitely lost some of its luster for me.

Most of this book has been about building *clarity* into Web sites: making sure that users can understand what it is they're looking at—and how to use it—without undue effort. Is it clear to people? Do they "get it"?

But there's another important component to Web usability: doing the right thing—being considerate of the user. Besides "Is my site clear?" you also need to be asking, "Does my site behave like a mensch?"

The Reservoir of Goodwill

I've always found it useful to imagine that every time we enter a Web site, we start out with a reservoir of goodwill. Each problem we encounter on the site lowers the level of that reservoir. Here, for example, is what my visit to the airline site might have looked like:

I enter the site.

My goodwill is a little low, because I'm not happy that their negotiations may seriously inconvenience me.

I glance around the Home page.

It feels well organized, so I relax a little. I'm confident that if the information is here, I'll be able to find it.

There's no mention of the strike on the Home page.

I don't like the fact that it feels like business as usual.

There's a list of five links to News stories on the Home page but none are relevant.

I click on the Press Releases link at the bottom of the list.

Latest press release is five days old.

I go to the About Us page.

No promising links, but plenty of promotions, which is very annoying. Why are they trying to sell me more tickets when I'm not sure they're going to fly me tomorrow?

I search for "strike" and find two press releases about a strike a year ago, and pages from the corporate history about a strike in the 1950s.

At this point, I would like to leave, but they're the sole source for this information.

I look through their FAQ lists, then leave.

The reservoir is limited, and if you treat users badly enough and exhaust it there's a good chance that they'll leave. But leaving isn't the only possible negative outcome; they may just not be as eager to use your site in the future, or they may think less of your organization.

There are a few things worth noting about this reservoir:

> **It's idiosyncratic.** Some people have a large reservoir, some small. Some people are more suspicious by nature, or more ornery; others are inherently more patient, trusting, or optimistic. The point is, you can't count on a very large reserve.

> **It's situational**. If I'm in a huge hurry, or have just come from a bad experience on another site, my expendable goodwill may already be low when I enter your site, even if I naturally have a large reserve.

> **You can refill it.** Even if you've made mistakes that have diminished my goodwill, you can replenish it by doing things that make me feel like you're looking out for my best interests.

> **Sometimes a single mistake can empty it.** For instance, just opening up a registration form with tons of fields may be enough to cause some people's reserve to plunge instantly to zero.

Things that diminish goodwill

Here are a few of the things that tend to make users feel like the people publishing a site don't have their best interests at heart:

 Hiding information that I want. The most common things to hide are customer support phone numbers, shipping rates, and prices.

The whole point of hiding support phone numbers is to try to keep users from calling, because each call costs money. The usual effect is to diminish goodwill and ensure that they'll be even more annoyed when they do find the number and call. On the other hand, if the 800 number is in plain sight—perhaps even on every page—somehow knowing that they *can* call if they want to is often enough to keep people looking for the information on the site longer, increasing the chances that they'll solve the problem themselves.

Some sites hide pricing information in hopes of getting users so far into the process that they'll feel vested in it by the time they experience the "sticker shock." My favorite example is Web sites for wireless access in public places like airports. Having seen a "Wireless access available!" sign and knowing that it's free at some airports, you open up your laptop, find a signal, and try to connect. But then you have to scan, read, and click your way through three pages, following links like "Wireless Access" and "Click here to connect" before you get to a page that even hints at what it might cost you. It feels like an old phone sales tactic: If they can just keep you on the line long enough and keep throwing more of their marketing pitch at you, maybe they can convince you along the way.

 Punishing me for not doing things your way. I should *never* have to think about formatting data: whether or not to put dashes in my Social Security number, spaces in my credit card number, or parentheses in my phone number. Many sites perversely insist on no spaces in credit card numbers, when the spaces actually make it much easier to get the number right. Don't make me jump through hoops just because you don't want to write a little bit of code.

Asking me for information you don't really need. Most users are very skeptical of requests for personal information, and find it annoying if a site asks for more than what's needed for the task at hand.

 Shucking and jiving me. We're always on the lookout for faux sincerity, and disingenuous attempts to convince me that you care about me can be particularly annoying. Think about what goes through *your* head every time you hear "Your call is important to us."

> Right. That's why your "unusually high call volume" is keeping me on hold for 20 minutes: because my call is important to you, but my time isn't.

 Putting sizzle in my way. Having to wait through a long Flash intro, or wade through pages bloated with feel-good marketing photos makes it clear that you don't understand—or care—that I'm in a hurry.

 Your site looks amateurish. You can lose goodwill if your site looks sloppy, disorganized, or unprofessional, like *no* effort has gone into making it presentable.

Note that while people love to make comments about the appearance of sites—especially about whether they like the colors—almost no one is going to leave a site just because it doesn't look *great*. (I tell people to ignore all comments that users make about colors during a user test, unless three out of four people use a word like "puke" to describe the color scheme. Then it's worth rethinking.[2])

There may be times when you'll choose to have your site do some of these user-unfriendly things deliberately. Sometimes it makes business sense not to do exactly what the customer wants. For instance, uninvited pop-ups almost always annoy people to some extent. But if your statistics show you can get 10 percent more revenue by using pop-ups and you think it's worth annoying your users, you can do it. It's a business decision. Just be sure you do it in an informed way, rather than inadvertently.

---

[2] *This actually happened once during a round of testing I facilitated. We changed the color.*

Things that increase goodwill

The good news is that even if you make mistakes, it's possible to restore my goodwill by doing things that convince me that you *do* have my interests at heart. Most of these are just the flip side of the other list:

Know the main things that people want to do on your site and make them obvious and easy. It's usually not hard to figure out what people want to do on a given Web site. I find that even people who disagree about everything else about their organization's site almost always give me the same answer when I ask them "What are the three main things your users want to do?" The problem is, making those things easy doesn't always become the top priority it should be. (If most people are coming to your site to apply for a mortgage, nothing should get in the way of making it dead easy to apply for a mortgage.)

Tell me what I want to know. Be upfront about things like shipping costs, hotel daily parking fees, service outages—anything you'd rather *not* be upfront about. You may lose points if your shipping rates are higher than I'd like, but you'll often gain enough points for candor and for making it easy for me to make up the difference.

Save me steps wherever you can. For instance, instead of giving me the shipping company's tracking number for my purchase, put a link in my email receipt that opens their site and submits my tracking number when I click it. (As usual, Amazon was the first site to do this for me.)

Put effort into it. My favorite example is the HP technical support site, where it seems like an enormous amount of work has gone into (a) generating the information I need to solve my problems, (b) making sure that it's accurate and useful, (c) presenting it clearly, and (d) organizing it so I can find it. I've had a lot of HP printers, and in almost every case where I've had a problem I've been able to solve it on my own.

Know what questions I'm likely to have, and answer them. Frequently Asked Questions lists are enormously valuable, especially if

> They really are FAQs, not marketing pitches masquerading as FAQs (also known as QWWPWAs: Questions We *Wish* People Would Ask).

> You keep them up to date. Customer Service and Technical Support can easily give you a list of this week's five most frequently asked questions. I would always put this list at the top of any site's Support page.

> They're candid. Often people are looking in the FAQs for the answer to a question you'd rather they hadn't asked. Candor in these situations goes a *long* way to increasing goodwill.

Provide me with creature comforts like printer-friendly pages. People love being able to print stories that span multiple pages with a single click, and CSS makes it relatively easy to create printer-friendly pages with little additional effort. Drop the ads (the possibility of a banner ad having any impact other than being annoying is even *greater* when it's just taking up space on paper), but *don't* drop the illustrations, photos, and figures.

Make it easy to recover from errors. If you actually do enough user testing, you'll be able to spare me from many errors before they happen. But where the potential for errors is unavoidable, always provide a graceful, obvious way for me to recover. See *Defensive Design for the Web* in my Recommended Reading for excellent advice on the subject.

When in doubt, apologize. Sometimes you can't help it: You just don't have the ability or resources to do what the user wants (for instance, your university's library system requires separate passwords for each of your catalog databases, so you can't give users the single log-in they'd like). If you can't do what they want, at least let them know that *you* know you're inconveniencing them.

Accessibility, Cascading Style Sheets, and you

JUST WHEN YOU THINK YOU'RE DONE, A CAT FLOATS
BY WITH BUTTERED TOAST STRAPPED TO ITS BACK

When a cat is dropped, it always lands on its feet, and when toast is dropped, it always lands with the buttered side facing down. I propose to strap buttered toast to the back of a cat; the two will hover, spinning, inches above the ground. With a giant buttered-cat array, a high-speed monorail could easily link New York with Chicago.

—JOHN FRAZEE, IN *THE JOURNAL OF IRREPRODUCIBLE RESULTS*

People sometimes ask me, "What about accessibility? Isn't that part of usability?"

And they're right, of course. Unless you're going to make a blanket decision that people with disabilities aren't part of your audience, you really can't say your site is usable unless it's accessible.

At this point,[1] everyone involved in Web design knows at least a little bit about Web accessibility, even if it's only that there's something special about the number 508.[2] And yet almost every site I go to fails my three-second accessibility test—increasing the size of the type.

Browser "Text Size" command

Before   After (no difference)

Why is that?

---

[1] *2005 AD*

[2] *In case you've literally been hiding under a rock for the past few years, "508" refers to Section 508 of the 1988 Amendments to the Rehabilitation Act, which specifies accessibility standards for information technology (like Web sites) that must be met by any vendor that wants to do business with the U.S. government.*

What developers and designers hear

In most organizations, the people who end up being responsible for doing something about accessibility are the people who actually *build* the thing: the designers and the developers.

When they try to learn about what they should do, whatever books or articles they pick up inevitably list the same set of reasons why they need to make their sites accessible:

There's a lot of truth in all of these. Unfortunately, there's also a lot that's unlikely to convince 26-year-old developers and designers that they should be "doing accessibility." Two arguments in particular tend to make them skeptical:

> Since their world consists largely of able-bodied 26-year-olds, it's very hard for them to believe that a large percentage of the population actually needs help accessing the Web. They're willing to write it off as the kind of exaggeration that people make when they're advocating for a worthy cause, but there's also a natural inclination to think, "If I can poke a hole in one of their arguments, I'm entitled to be skeptical about the rest."

> They're also skeptical about the idea that making things more accessible benefits everyone. Some adaptations do, like the classic example, closed captioning, which does often come in handy for people who can hear.[3] But since this always seems to be the only example cited, it feels a little like arguing

---

[3] *Melanie and I often use it when watching British films, for instance.*

that the space program was worthwhile because it gave us Tang.[4] It's much easier for developers and designers to imagine cases where accessibility adaptations are likely to make things *worse* for "everyone else."

The worst thing about this skepticism is that it obscures the fact that there's really only one reason that's important:

> It's the right thing to do.

And not just the right thing; it's *profoundly* the right thing to do, because the one argument for accessibility that doesn't get made nearly often enough is how extraordinarily better it makes some people's lives. Personally, I don't think anyone should need more than this one example: Blind people with access to a computer can now read the daily newspaper on their own. Imagine that.

How many opportunities do we have to dramatically improve people's lives just by doing our job a little better?

And for those of you who don't find this argument compelling, be aware that there will be a legislative stick coming sooner or later. Count on it.

What designers and developers fear

As they learn more about accessibility, two fears tend to emerge:

> **More work**. For developers in particular, accessibility can seem like just one more complicated new thing to fit into an already impossible project schedule. In the worst case, it gets handed down as an "initiative" from above, complete with time-consuming reports, reviews, and task force meetings.

> **Compromised design.** What designers fear most is what I refer to as buttered cats: places where good design for people with disabilities and good design for everyone else are going to be in direct opposition. They're worried that they're going to be forced to design sites that are less appealing—and less useful—for the majority of their audience.

---

[4] *A powdered orange-flavored breakfast drink, invented for the astronauts (see also: freeze-dried food).*

In an ideal world, accessibility would work like a sign I saw in the back of a Chicago taxi. At first it looked like an ordinary sign. But something about the way it caught the light made me take a closer look, and when I did, I realized that it was ingenious.

The sign was overlaid with a thin piece of Plexiglas, and the message was embossed in Braille on the Plexiglas. Ordinarily, both the print and the Braille would have been half as large so they could both fit on the sign, but with this design each audience got the best possible experience. It was an elegant solution.

I think for some designers, though, accessibility conjures up an image something like the Vonnegut short story where the government creates equality by handicapping everyone.[5]

The real solution—as usual—is a few years away

When people start reading about accessibility, they usually come across one piece of advice that sounds very promising:

---

[5] In "Harrison Bergeron," the main character, whose intelligence is "way above normal," is required by law to wear a "mental handicap radio" in his ear that blasts various loud noises every 20 seconds "to keep people like George from taking unfair advantage of their brains."

The problem is, when they run their site through a validator, it turns out to be more like a grammar checker than a spell checker. Yes, it does find some obvious mistakes and oversights that are easy to fix, like missing alt text.[6] But it also inevitably turns up a series of vague warnings that you *may* be doing something wrong, and a long list of recommendations of things for you to check which it admits may *not* be problems at all.

This can be very discouraging for people who are just learning about accessibility, because the long lists and ambiguous advice suggest that there's an awful lot to learn.

And the truth is, it's a lot harder than it ought to be to make a site accessible.

After all, most designers and developers are not going to become accessibility experts. If Web accessibility is going to become ubiquitous, it's going to have to be easier to do. Screen readers and other adaptive technologies have to get smarter, the tools for building sites (like Macromedia Dreamweaver) have to make it easier to code correctly for accessibility, and the guidelines need to be improved.

---

[6] *Alt text provides a text description of an image ("Picture of two men on a sailboat," for example), which is essential for people using screen readers or browsing with images turned off.*

Real progress is going to require improvements on four different fronts, motivated by things like profit incentive, the threat of lawsuits and legislation, and the desire to support mobile devices, which share some problems with accessibility.

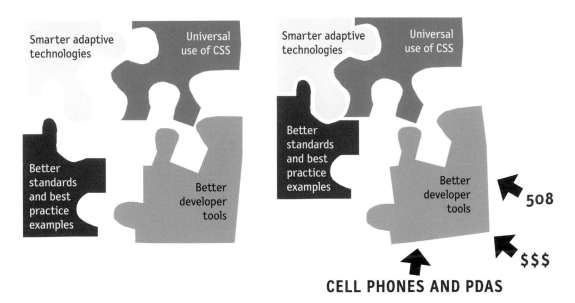

The five things you can do right now

The fact that it's not a perfect world at the moment doesn't let any of us off the hook, though.

Even with current technology and standards, it's possible to make any site very accessible without an awful lot of effort by focusing on a few things that will have the most impact. And they don't involve getting anywhere near a buttered cat.

#1. Fix the usability problems that confuse everyone

One of the things that I find annoying about the Tang argument ("making sites accessible makes them more usable for everyone") is that it obscures the fact that the reverse actually *is* true: Making sites more usable for "the rest of us" is one of the most effective ways to make them more effective for people with disabilities.

If something confuses most people who use your site, it's almost certain to confuse users who have accessibility issues. (They don't suddenly become remarkably smarter because they have a disability.) And it's very likely that they're going to have a harder time recovering from their confusion.

For instance, think of the last time you had trouble using a Web site (running into a confusing error message when you submitted a form, for instance). Now imagine trying to solve that problem without being able to see the page.

The single best thing you can do to improve your site's accessibility is to test it often, and continually smooth out the parts that confuse everyone. In fact, if you don't do this first, no matter how rigorously you apply accessibility guidelines, people with disabilities still won't be able to use it. If your site's not clear to begin with, making it Bobby-compliant is like [insert your favorite putting-lipstick-on-a-pig metaphor here].

#2. Read an article

As I hope you've seen by now, the best way to learn how to make anything more usable is to watch people actually try to use it. But most of us have no experience at using adaptive technology, let alone watching other people use it.

If you had the time and the motivation, I'd highly recommend locating one or two blind Web users and spending a few hours with them observing how they actually use their screen reader software.

Fortunately, someone has done the heavy lifting for you. Mary Theofanos and Janice (Ginny) Redish watched 16 blind users using screen readers to do a number of tasks on a variety of sites and reported what they observed in an article titled "Guidelines for Accessible and Usable Web Sites: Observing Users Who Work with Screen Readers."[7]

As with any kind of user testing, it produced invaluable insights. Here's one example of the kinds of things they learned:

---

[7] *Published in the ACM Magazine,* Interactions *(November-December 2003). With permission from ACM, Ginny has made it available for personal use at* http://redish.net/content/papers/interactions.html.

Screen-reader users scan with their ears. Most blind users are just as impatient as most sighted users. They want to get the information they need as quickly as possible. They do not listen to every word on the page—just as sighted users do not read every word. They "scan with their ears," listening to just enough to decide whether to listen further. Many set the voice to speak at an amazingly rapid rate.

They listen to the first few words of a link or line of text. If it does not seem relevant, they move quickly to the next link, next line, next heading, next paragraph. Where a sighted user might find a keyword by scanning over the entire page, a blind user may not hear that keyword if it is not at the beginning of a link or a line of text.

I highly recommend that you read this article before you read anything else about accessibility. In 20 minutes, it will give you an appreciation for the problems you're trying to solve that you won't get from any other articles or books.

#3. Read a book

After you've read Ginny and Mary's article, you're ready to spend a day (or a weekend) reading a book about Web accessibility. There are several good ones...

> *Building Accessible Websites* by Joe Clark

> *Constructing Accessible Websites* by Jim Thatcher et al.

> *Maximum Accessibility: Making Your Web Site More Usable for Everyone* by John Slatin and Sharron Rush

> A CD-ROM called *The WebAIM Guide to Web Accessibility Techniques and Concepts*

...and I'm sure there will be more in the near future.[8]

These books cover a lot of ground, so don't worry about absorbing all of it. For now, you just need to get the big picture.

---

[8] *I'll keep an updated list of recommendations on my Web site.*

#4. Start using Cascading Style Sheets

First, a little Web history.

In the beginning, everything was text. When the first visual browsers arrived, designers found that unlike desktop publishing, which gave them control of *everything,* HTML—which was really only intended to display research papers—gave them almost no control over anything. Commands for styling text were crude, and it was very hard to position things precisely on a page. And even if you could, pages often looked completely different when viewed in different browsers.

To wrestle back some control, designers and developers started using tables to control layout. For years, the only way to control the position of things on a Web page was to put them in tables... and tables within tables. Most pages ended up seeming like a series of Russian nesting dolls.

Unfortunately, this didn't work well with early screen readers, which tended to read rather slavishly line-by-line from left to right, like this:

> Advanced Common Sense can't afford a consultant here's is the online home of web everything I know about web usability...

Advanced Common Sense^{sm} is the online home of Web usability consultant Steve Krug. I specialize in **The book!** Can't afford a consultant? Here's everything I know about Web usability (well, almost everything) in 208 pages.

They also started using various HTML commands in ways they weren't meant to be used, to try to get more control over text styling. It was a messy world of hacks, held together with chewing gum.

Fortunately, beginning in 1998 some very determined people got fed up with this state of affairs, and decided to convince browser manufacturers to support Web standards that would give designers a consistent target. A group of designers calling themselves The Web Standards Project employed a brilliant form of nonviolent resistance: They simply stopped making their own sites backwardly compatible with browsers that didn't support standards like CSS, and encouraged others to do the same.

Several year later, CSS Zen Garden[9] (a single HTML page that looked completely different depending on which of the many designer-contributed style sheets you applied to it) demonstrated that you could create beautiful, sophisticated designs with CSS.

Cascading Style Sheets are now so well supported by most browsers that it doesn't make any sense to create a site without them, because the advantages are enormous:

> **Infinitely greater control of formatting.**

> **Flexibility.** A single change in a style sheet can change the appearance of an entire site, or automatically generate useful variations like printer-friendly pages.

> **Consistency among browsers.** Workarounds and hacks are still required to ensure that your CSS works across all browsers, but these will fall away as browser makers continue to improve their CSS support.

And implementing CSS will make it easy for you to do two things that will greatly improve your site's accessibility:

> **Serialize your content.** Unlike table-based layout, with CSS you can put your content in sequential order in the source file—which is how a screen reader user will hear it—and still position things where you want them on the page.

> **Allow your text to resize.** CSS makes it easy to make your text resizable, which is enormously helpful for low-vision users (and people old enough to need bifocals).

---

[9] www.csszengarden.com. *See* The Zen of CSS Design *by Dave Shea and Molly Holzschlag (New Riders, 2005) for a great description of the project.*

Probably the fastest way to learn CSS is to get someone who specializes in it to do a "markover" for you—recoding a few of your site's page templates to use CSS—and learn by watching them do it. When you're ready, there are also a number of good books on CSS, especially the ones by Eric Meyer.

#5. Go for the low-hanging fruit

Now you're ready to do what most people think of as Web accessibility: implementing specific changes in your HTML code.

As of right now, these are probably the most important things to do:

> **Add appropriate alt text to every image.** Add an alt attribute for images that screen readers should ignore, and add helpful, descriptive text for the rest. All of the Web accessibility books have very good explanations of how to do this.

> **Make your forms work with screen readers.** This largely boils down to using the HTML label element to associate the fields with their prompts, so people know what they're supposed to enter.

> **Create a "Skip to Main Content" link at the beginning of each page.** Imagine having to spend 20 seconds (or a minute, or two) listening to the global navigation at the top of every page before you could look at the content, and you'll understand why this is important.

> **Make all content accessible by keyboard.** Remember, not everyone can use a mouse.

> **Don't use JavaScript without a good reason.** Some adaptive technologies don't support it very well yet.

> **Use client-side (*not* server-side) image maps.** Alt tags don't work with server-side image maps.

That's it. You'll probably learn how to do a lot more as you go along, but even if you only do what I've covered here, you'll be doing a pretty good job.

Hopefully in five years I'll be able to just remove this chapter and use the space for something else because the developer tools, browsers, screen readers, and guidelines will all have matured and will be integrated to the point where people can build accessible sites without thinking about it.

12

Help! My boss wants me to _____.

WHEN BAD DESIGN DECISIONS HAPPEN TO GOOD PEOPLE

W HEN I TEACH MY WEB USABILITY WORKSHOPS, I've noticed that a lot of the questions people ask take this form:

> Help! My boss (or "My marketing manager," or "Our CEO") wants me to _____.

For instance, "My marketing manager insists that we make people provide their postal mailing address before we send them our email newsletter! What can I do?"

Two of these questions about usability disasters imposed from above tend to come up over and over:

> My boss wants us to ask users for more personal information than we really need.

> My boss wants our site to have more "pizazz" (read: splash pages, animation, music, etc., etc.) .

I've reached the point where when people ask me either of these questions, I'll often say—half jokingly—that if it will help I'll be happy to write their boss an email (from a usability "expert"—with a book, no less) explaining why this is a really bad idea.

Here are the emails. Feel free to use them as you see fit.

The perils of asking for too much personal data

From: Steve Krug (skrug@sensible.com)

To: [yourboss@youremployer.com]

At my recent Web usability workshop in [*name of city*], your Web [designer|developer|manager] [*your name*] asked my advice about how much personal information you should ask for on a registration form. I offered to send you email recapping my advice to him.

Anyone who uses the Web has run into this many times: You decide to subscribe to an email newsletter (or request a free sample, register a product, or create an acount). Anything that involves you providing information about yourself and getting something in return.

You click "Subscribe" and a form appears. It looks longer than you expected, and you quickly discover why. For no good reason, you're being asked to provide your mailing address. And your phone number. And your occupation. Suddenly, quick task has become a project.

Usability professionals have a technical term for this practice. It's what we call "a very bad idea."

I can understand that it's tempting to try to get as much personal data as you can, given the uses you can put it to. The problem is that people filling in any kind of form on the Web are always asking themselves, "Why are they asking me for this piece of information? Do they really need it to give me what I want?" If the answer is no, then the next question is, "Then what do they want it for?"

In most people's minds there are only are two possible explanations: either (a) you're so clueless about the Web that you don't know that they find this offensive, or (b) you do know, but you want the information badly for some other purpose, and you don't mind offending them to get it.

As a result, there are three serious downsides to asking for more than what you need:

- **It tends to keep you from getting real data.** As soon as people realize you're asking for more than you need, they feel completely justified in lying to you. I often tell my clients that email addresses are like heroin to marketing people—so addictive that it doesn't strike them as odd that 10% of their subscribers happen to be named "Barney Rubble."

- **You get fewer completed forms.** The formula is simple: the less data you ask for, the more submissions you'll get. People tend to be in an enormous hurry on the Web, and if the form looks even a little bit longer than they expect, many just won't bother.

- **It makes you look bad.** People who really want your newsletter may jump through whatever hoops they have to, but make no mistake: it will diminish their impression of you while they're doing it. On the other hand, if you only ask for the information you need, you've established a relationship with them and can get more data later in subsequent exchanges.

Here are three guidelines:

- Only make me provide what you need to complete this transaction.

- Don't ask for a lot of *optional* information, either. Just the sight of a lot of fields is depressing. Asking for fewer optional items will get you more replies.

- Show me the value I'm going to receive in exchange for my information. Tell me exactly what I'll get by registering, show me a sample of the newsletter, etc.

I hope this is helpful. By the way, based on the brief chance I had to chat with [*your name*], [he|she] seems to be an excellent [designer|developer|manager]. You're lucky to have [him|her] on your team.

Steve Krug
Author of *Don't Make Me Think! A Common Sense Approach to Web Usability*

Adding "sizzle" to your Web site

From: Steve Krug (skrug@sensible.com)

To: [yourboss@youremployer.com]

Your Web [designer|developer|manager], [*your name*], recently attended one of my Web usability workshops and asked my advice about your plans to make your site [more visually interesting|more engaging] by adding [a splash page|some animation|large photos|background music].

I told [him|her] I'd be happy to pass along some of the advice I give to my own executive clients when they make similar requests of their Web teams.

Unfortunately, there's an inherent problem with the way executives are involved in Web site design. Given that the site is crucial to your organization, naturally your input is solicited. But because of the way sites are developed, all you're really asked to comment on is the *appearance* of the site, based on a few preliminary designs. Given what you have to go on, the only thing you can reasonably judge is "Does it look good to me?" and "Does it create a good impression?" As a result, CEO's almost always push for something that's more visually appealing, something with more "pizzazz" or "sizzle."

The problem is that except in a few specific cases—which I'll get to in a minute—Web sites don't really need much sizzle. Yes, looks do count. Yes, it has to look presentable, professional, and attractive. But "flashy"? "Engaging"? Almost never.

Most of the time on the Web, people don't *want* to be engaged; they just want to get something *done*, and attempts to engage them that interfere with their current mission are perceived as annoying, clueless, and the worst kind of hucksterism. And attempts to add sizzle almost always get in their way. I won't bother cataloging all the problems with all the different forms of sizzle: Splash pages that signal you as several years behind the times. Big photos that take a long time to load (have you ever used your own site from a hotel room?) and leave less room on the page for what people are looking for. And distracting music and animation that most people can't stand.

Unless your site gives people the information they want and makes it easy for them to do what you want them to, the main thing it's doing is announcing that you're either clueless about the Web, or you care more about your image than you do about them.

Of course there are exceptions. There are some sites where sizzle makes sense, sites where what you're selling is sizzle: entertainment sites (for music, movies, etc.), pure branding sites (for a breakfast cereal, for instance), and portfolio sites for Web developers. But if your site isn't on that list, most sizzle is going to be counterproductive.

The moral is, you can do as much as you want to make your site *look good*, but only if it's not at the expense of making it *work well*. And most sizzle gets in the way of it working well.

Think about your own experience: the sites you enjoy using. Is it because they're "flashy," or because they have content you want or need? Can you name a site that has content that's interesting or useful to you that you *don't* use because it's not visually interesting enough?

I hope this helps.

By the way, you're lucky to have [*your name*] on your Web team. [He|she] really knows [his|her] stuff.

Steve Krug
Author of *Don't Make Me Think! A Common Sense Approach to Web Usability*

Never say never

Just one caution: Note that I'm not saying you should never do any of these things. If there's one thing you learn by working on a lot of different Web sites, it's that almost any design idea—no matter how appallingly bad—can be made usable in the right circumstances, with enough effort. And almost any good design idea can be made unusable, by messing up the details of the implementation.

But the things I'm talking about here are generally very bad practices, and you shouldn't be doing any of them unless (a) you really know what you're doing, (b) you have a darned good reason, and (c) you actually are going to test it when you're done to make sure you've managed to make it work; you're not just going to intend to test it.

Also, realize that your boss is probably not just being perverse. There is almost always a good (or at least not-so-awful) intention lurking behind insistence on a bad design idea. Trying to understand that good intention is often the best way to figure out how to make your case for a different approach.

That's all, folks

As Bob and Ray used to say, "Hang by your thumbs, and write if you get work." I hope you'll check in at my Web site www.sensible.com from time to time.

But above all, be of good cheer. As I said at the beginning, building a great Web site is an enormous challenge, and anyone who gets it even half right has my admiration.

And please don't take anything I've said as being against breaking "the rules"—or at least bending them. I know there are even sites where you want the interface to make people think, to puzzle or challenge them. Just be sure you know which rules you're bending, and that you at least *think* you have a good reason for bending them.

Recommended reading

THERE ARE DOZENS OF WORTHWHILE USABILITY-RELATED books and Web sites I *could* recommend, but these are the ones that have really influenced the way I think about the Web.

> INFORMATION ARCHITECTURE FOR THE WORLD WIDE WEB

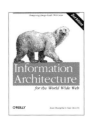

Louis Rosenfeld and Peter Morville, O'Reilly, 2nd Edition, 2002
Hands down, the single most useful book about Web site design. They tackle the issues of navigation, labeling, and searching with admirable clarity and practicality.

> WHY WE BUY: THE SCIENCE OF SHOPPING

Paco Underhill, Simon and Schuster, 2000
A wonderful summary of many years of detailed observation of shoppers in their natural habitat. Even though the subject is the brick-and-mortar shopping experience, the problem is the same as Web design: creating complex, engaging environments where people look for things—and find them.

> SOURCES OF POWER: HOW PEOPLE MAKE DECISIONS

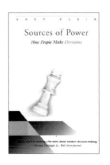

Gary Klein, MIT Press, 1999
Klein's study of naturalistic decision making is another wonderful example of how field observation can reveal the difference between the way we think we do things and the way we actually do them. If the *Whole Earth Catalog* still existed, this book and *Why We Buy* would both be in it.

> ### THE PRACTICE OF CREATIVITY: A MANUAL FOR DYNAMIC GROUP PROBLEM SOLVING
> *George M. Prince*, Macmillan, 1972.
> I took a course in the Synectics method thirty-five years ago, and there hasn't been a week since then that I haven't used something I learned from it. Think of it as brainstorming on steroids, coupled with some remarkable insights into how people work in groups. The book is out of print, but you can find a copy pretty easily via the Web.

> ### JAKOB NIELSEN'S WEB SITE, USEIT.COM (www.useit.com). Beginning with *Usability Engineering* in 1984, Jakob Nielsen has long been usability's most articulate and thought-provoking advocate. And since the advent of the Web, he's shown up everywhere but on milk cartons preaching the value of Web usability.
>
> I don't always agree with what he says, but I always admire the way he says it. His site houses his biweekly Alertbox columns (another reason to admire him: a columnist who's smart enough to know he doesn't have something important to say every week), and links to all of the best usability resources on the Web.
>
> Also check out his Nielsen Norman Group reports (www.nngroup.com/reports/). They may seem pricey (typically $100-$300), but they contain reliable information you won't find anywhere else on specific areas (like intranet usability) and specific audience segments (like children, seniors, and people with disabilities).

> ### HOMEPAGE USABILITY: 50 WEBSITES DECONSTRUCTED

Jakob Nielsen, Marie Tahir, New Riders, 2001

The bad news about this book is that after you've seen the problems of twenty-five Home pages, you've seen them all. The good news, though, is that the excellent set of 113 Home page design guidelines crammed into the first 28 pages is worth the price of the entire book.

> ### WEB APPLICATION DESIGN HANDBOOK: BEST PRACTICES FOR WEB-BASED SOFTWARE

Susan Fowler and Victor Stanwick, Morgan Kaufmann, 2004

Susan and Victor have written the *Junior Woodchucks Guidebook* of Web applications: Everything you need to know is in there, including tons of best practice examples, insights from years of experience, and assorted fascinating arcana. If you're designing or building Web applications, you'd be foolish not to have a copy.

> ### DEFENSIVE DESIGN FOR THE WEB

37 Signals, New Riders, 2004

The subtitle (*How to Improve Error Messages, Help, Forms, and Other Crisis Points*) says it all. An excellent, practical, *short* book—full of best practice examples—about how to design to prevent user errors from happening, and to help them recover painlessly when they do.

> ## THE DESIGN OF EVERYDAY THINGS

Don Norman, Basic Books, 2002

Originally published as *The Psychology of Everyday Things*, then renamed because designers weren't finding it in the Psychology department of bookstores, this actually *is* a usability classic. Because it was first published in 1984, you won't find any mention of the Web, but the principles are the same.

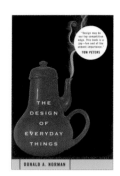

You'll never look at doorknobs the same way again.

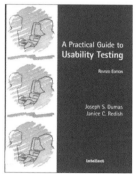

> ## A PRACTICAL GUIDE TO USABILITY TESTING

Joseph Dumas and Janice (Ginny) Redish, Intellect, 1999

The best how-to book out there on user testing, and my favorite—at least until I write the one I keep scribbling notes for.

Ginny is also currently writing a book on writing for the Web, which I can recommend highly, sight unseen.

In the same vein, *Caroline Jarrett* (www.formsthatwork.com/), whom I consider the authority on designing Web forms, is writing the definitive book on, well...designing Web forms. If it hasn't appeared by 2006, send her an email and pester her about it.

> ## USABILITY NEWS

http://psychology.wichita.edu/surl

This newsletter is my favorite source of usability research. Published twice a year by the Wichita State University Software Usability Research Laboratory (SURL), it always contains several very nice, bite-sized pieces of well-thought-out research. The full archives are available online.

> ## WebWord

http://www.webword.com/
John Rhodes

UsabilityViews.com

http://www.usabilityviews.com/
Chris McEvoy

These sites are currently the two best ways to keep up to date on everything that's being published online about usability. John Rhodes' WebWord is more of a true blog in that he comments on the articles he links to, but Chris McEvoy is dogged in tracking down everything worth looking at. Between the two of them, you won't miss anything.

> ## Usability.gov research-based guidelines

http://usability.gov/guidelines/index.html
This excellent set of Web design and usability guidelines, published by the National Cancer Institute (NCI), includes very nice examples and references to the research each guideline is based on.

If you have a usability question, it's always worth checking here first to see if they've covered it.

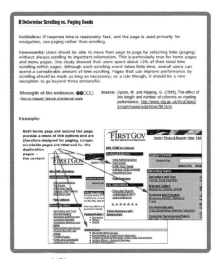

www.usability.gov

Acknowledgments

...AND ALL I GOT WAS THIS LOUSY T-SHIRT

D ON'T KID YOURSELF. A BOOK LIKE THIS IS LARGELY THE work of one person. There's no other single human being who's spent nearly as much time as I have thinking about it, perseverating over it, changing the same sentence back and forth between two different versions over and over.

But I get my name on the cover, where everyone else involved gets just slightly less than bupkus. And even if I'd had a million years to work on it, you'd never be reading this if it hadn't been for the talent, skill, encouragement, kindness, patience, generosity, and forbearance of many people.

Editors, designers, patrons, and enablers

I've always heard horror stories about stormy farmer/cowman relationships between authors and editors, but personally I love having a good editor tell me where I've gone astray. With a book—just as with a Web site—you don't have to work on it long before you're just too close to it to see things clearly. I was fortunate enough to have the benefit of two editors:

> **Karen Whitehouse** from Macmillan always thought this book was a good idea, always knew what I was trying to get at (even when I didn't), never rapped my knuckles (even when I deserved it), and was always a delight to be around. If you write a book, you should be so lucky. I will miss not having an excuse to talk to her all the time.

> **Barbara Flanagan**, a longtime friend and masterful copy editor who by her own admission can't even read a novel without a pencil in her hand, read the manuscript at several stages out of the goodness of her heart, in her copious spare time. She showed me elegant ways out of countless corners I had painted myself into.

Wherever you detect a flaw in this book, you should just imagine either Karen or Barbara—or both—saying, "Well, if you really insist...."

In designing this book, **Allison Cecil** knowingly took on a maniac's job.[1] Imagine designing a book for a nitpicking, opinionated author who's written a book espousing his own design principles and insists that the book has to reflect them. And naturally, in the grand *Beat the Clock* do-it-under-water tradition, it all had to be done in a nightmarishly small amount of time. She managed it only by (a) forgoing sleep—and everything else—for weeks on end with enormous good grace, and (b) displaying talent equal to her patience. As with Karen and Barbara, anything that strikes you as a design flaw is almost certainly something she did only because I twisted her arm.

David Matt and **Elizabeth Oh** at Roger Black Consulting and **Trina Wurst** and **Sandra Schroeder** at Macmillan made major contributions to the design and production, and **Mark Matcho** provided the illustrations in an ungodly rush.

Roger Black has generously encouraged my work for years now, and it's always a treat to work with him and watch the unique—and amusing—thought balloons that form over *his* head. The only downside is that I all-too-rarely get to enjoy the pleasure of his company because he's always in Uruguay or Singapore. It was his suggestion that I do this book in the first place, and he and **Jock Spivy** saw to it that Circle.com provided support that made it possible.

Alexandra Anderson-Spivy ("Ally") managed the project from Circle.com's end and provided valuable editorial advice and—as is her way—invaluable moral support from start to finish.

Sounding boards

I relied on many people to tell me whether I was actually making any sense, or just—in the words of Scotty the reporter in *The Thing from Another World*[2] — "stuffed full of wild blueberries." But I relied most heavily on my two best friends:

---

[1] cf. *Kevin Kline's explanation of his life as a fireman in* The January Man: *"Building's on fire, everybody runs out, you run in. It's a maniac's job."*

[2] *...the 1949 Howard Hawks original, not the John Carpenter remake.*

> **Paul Shakespear** spent many hours—hours when he could have been painting—reading drafts that barely made sense, things I could never have shown to anyone else, and telling me what to complete and what to throw overboard. The ensuing discussions were much more interesting than this book, as is always the case with Paul.

Little Wing
2004
59" x 28"
acrylic on wood

paulshakespear.com

> **Richard Gingras** knows more about online publishing and creating a positive user experience than anyone I know. His reaction to my first chapter was what enabled me to go on, as his friendship has made many things in my life possible. I finished writing this book while staying with Richard, his wife, **Mitzi Trumbo**, their daughter, **Molly**, and Mitzi's wonderful mother, **Cleo**, as I do whenever I'm working in Silicon Valley—my "other family," as my wife says. Their companionship means more to me than I can say here.

Many other people were generous enough to take time they didn't really have to read and comment on various drafts: **Sue Hay**, **Hilary Goodall**, **Peggy Redpath**, **Jennifer Fleming**, **Lou Rosenfeld**, **Robert Raines**, **Richard Saul Wurman**, **Jeff Veen**, **Donna Slote**, **Matt Stark**, **Christine Bauer**, **Bob Gower**, **Dan Roam**, **Peter Stoermer**, and **John Kenrick**. As is always the case with user testing, their reactions and suggestions improved the end result enormously.

In addition to reading drafts, **Cleo Huggins**—one of the finest designers I know, and one of the most pleasant and interesting people—made an outlandishly generous offer of help when I needed it most.

Gail Blumberg was my problem-solving "lifeline" through this whole process, steering me safely through every situation that required finesse or any sense of politics and making me laugh while she did it. At this point, I owe her so many dinners for so many favors that I think I have to buy her a restaurant.

My next-door neighbor, graphic designer **Courtney McGlynn**—who has cheerfully played the role of "average user" on short notice over the years whenever I've needed to do a quick user test—helped me think through some vexing design issues.

Mentors

Dave Flanagan, **John Kirsch**, and **Jon Hirschtick** taught me by their example that hard-nosed business and extraordinary decency are not incompatible, which enabled me to be comfortable working as a consultant. John also dragged me kicking and screaming into professional adulthood at no small personal expense, standing by patiently while I learned to write something longer than a page—a gift I can never repay. **Pete Johnson** improved this book enormously without even looking at it—just by showing me by his example over the years what really good writing is.

Clients, co-workers, clients-turned-friends, and co-workers-turned-friends

Much of what I know about Web usability came from working with many smart, talented people like **Arwyn Bryant**, **Jim Albrecht**, **John Lennon**, **John Goecke**, **Jim Kent**, **Bill McCall**, **Dan Roam**, **James Caldwell**, **John Lyle Sanford**, **Lucie Soublin**, **Peter Karnig**, and **Theo Fels**.

Family

My brother **Phil Krug** has been there for me all my life, not counting the early years of holding me down and tickling me.

My son **Harry** was enormously patient while I was writing this, even when it meant turning down the sound on his computer while he played *Midtown Madness*. Lately, he's assumed the role of nine-year-old press agent, taking the manuscript along to our local Barnes & Noble to see how it would look on the shelf, creating a cover for it when we needed one, and declaring it a good read.

My wife **Melanie Sokol** has told me for a long time now that I'd better not say anywhere in the book that she was supportive. The truth is, she was incredibly supportive during the four months the book was *supposed* to take, and even during the next four months. And it wasn't even the third four months that did it; it was little things, like the fact that I apparently had no idea when—if ever—I *would* be finished. She knows how grateful I am.

Other

Flo and the crew at **Brueggers' Bagel Bakery** in West Roxbury never made me feel like a nuisance in all the mornings I occupied a table for hours on end, nursing a cup of coffee, scrawling on countless pieces of paper, and staring off into space.

Being a bear of little brain, I know I've overlooked someone; probably you. Hopefully, by the time you read this, your T-shirt will be in the mail.

Update: The Second Edition

I consider myself very fortunate that when I went to round up the usual suspects—**Karen Whitehouse**, **Allison Cecil** (if you need a book designed, find her!), **Paul Shakespear**, **Barbara Flanagan** and **Roger Black**—they all graciously agreed to help again.

Once again **Harry** and **Melanie** have put up with me in writing mode (never a pretty picture), while making it all worthwhile.

Several people were very generous in sharing their knowledge with me, including **Ginny Redish**, **Jeffrey Zeldman**, **Eric Meyer**, **Caroline Jarrett**, **Carol Barnum**, and **Lou Rosenfeld**, my workshop traveling companion, and now good friend.

Harry Krug, circa 2005

Thanks to the folks at Peachpit, **Nancy Ruenzel**, **Marjorie Baer**, Lisa Brazieal, **Kim Lombardi**, and the rest, and particularly to **Rachel Charlton Tiley** (and **Kathy Malmloff** before her) who fielded scores of book-related questions and requests with great patience over the years.

The coffee this time was from the Putterham Circle **Starbucks** in Brookline. They have really good fruit salad—firm grapes being the key—and they've been just as hospitable as the folks at Brueggers' were last time around.

Finally, to everyone who's written me or said hello in person because of the book, thank you. It's been a pleasure.

Index